Sons of Purpose

a View of Biblical Heroes through the Eyes of 21st Century Men

a 40 Writer Collaboration
Volume 2

Sons of Purpose

a View of Biblical Heroes through the Eyes of 21st Century Men

a 40 Writer Collaboration
Volume 2

Chris Hunter, Jr.

including 39 Contributing Writers

To order products, or for any other correspondence:

Hunter Entertainment Network
Colorado Springs, Colorado 80840
www.hunter-ent-net.com
Tel. (253) 906-2160
E-mail: contact@hunter-entertainment.com
Or reach us on Facebook & Instagram at: Hunter Entertainment Network
"Offering God's Heart to a Dying World"

This book and all other Hunter Entertainment Network™ Hunter Heart Publishing™, and Hunter Heart Kids™ books are available at Christian bookstores and distributors worldwide.

Chief Editor: Deborah G. Hunter
Book cover design: Phil Coles Independent Design
Layout & logos: Exousia Marketing Group www.exousiamg.com

ISBN: 978-1-937741-07-5
Printed in the United States of America.

Dedication

In every generation, God raises up fearless men that will take their rightful place in leadership. We live in an hour where it is absolutely imperative that men step into their divine purpose as sons of God. This devotional goes out to all the men across the Earth that desire to be nothing less than everything that God has called you to be. May the men of the Bible that are revealed through this devotional, with real time testimonies, become a spiritual blueprint on how to live as a Godly man in the last days.

Table of Contents

Introduction

The Bible was written over 2000 years ago. Over the centuries, we have come to grow extremely fond of the biblical characters we have been introduced to by some of the greatest scribes in history. Within the biblical stories of these men, we are afforded a front row seat to peer into their lives: good, bad, ugly, or indifferent. We are able to learn from their lessons, discern through their difficulties, and wield from the wisdom shared not only at the hands of the writers, but also through the breath and voice of the Spirit of the Living God. These life stories that we were graced by the Lord to experience were breathed on and inspired by the very life-giving Holy Spirit, the Ruach HaKodesh. Each and every man mentioned in the Bible is of great significance, even if only his name is written.

God speaks nothing haphazardly. Every word, and yes, every name spoken, reflects and reveals something of great importance to our heavenly Father. As you journey through this devotional, *Sons of Purpose, a View of Biblical Heroes through the Eyes of 21st Century Men, Volume 2,* utilize your heavenly imagination and travel back through biblical times to get to know these amazing men of the Bible. Read, study, and meditate upon their lives so you are able to understand their significance of being included, and how their lives tie into the birth, life, death, burial, and resurrection of our Lord and Savior, the Messiah, Jesus the Christ. Also, witness how ordinary, yet profound, men of the 21st Century parallel their lives to their biblical heroes.

"And they overcame him by the blood of the Lamb and by the word of their testimony, and they did not love their lives to the death." Revelation 12:11

CHRIS HUNTER, JR.

Your testimony is one of the most powerful evangelistic tools you can possess! As you read these transparent and compelling stories, allow the Spirit of God to ignite His fire within you to go into all the world to share with others what He has done for you! You are a *Son of Purpose!*

Saul

Chris Hunter, Jr.

"Then Saul, still breathing threats and murder against the disciples of the Lord, went to the high priest and asked letters from him to the synagogues of Damascus, so that if he found any who were of the Way, whether men or women, he might bring them bound to Jerusalem." Acts 9:1-2

I was raised in a Christian home all of my childhood and teenage life. Upon graduating high school and entering the United States Army, I converted to Islam. I was searching to fill a void that was evident in my life. From as early on as I can remember, I would hear my dad and family members, along with friends of theirs, talk about the atrocities committed against our people... people of color... African Americans. I was born in the early 70s, so we were just coming out of the Civil Rights Era of the 60s. The names I heard of most of my childhood were Martin Luther King, Jr., Malcolm X, Huey P. Newton, Marcus Garvey, along with the Black Panther Party and the NAACP.

You can imagine me growing up in a Christian church with a "white Jesus" image hanging up in our home, while listening to stories of the KKK lynching black people and how "white men" enslaved people of color for over 400 years. My young mind could not fathom, or grasp, serving a "white God" that would allow the people He created to be enslaved. As I entered high school, I became very angry and rebellious against the *religion* of Christianity, because I would hear how these "white men" from Europe brought Christianity to the New World along with millions of slaves from the coasts of Africa. How could this be? How could those claiming to serve the one true God of Heaven, the God of love, kidnap people from their homeland, put them in chains, and transport them on ships across the ocean where many never made it alive? On ships where they were packed like sardines, in chains, on top of one another, while lying in urine and feces, starving and dehydrated. You get the picture, right?

I struggled greatly trying to read the Bible and to find myself in its pages. The only scriptures I could find took me to the Old Testament where the Israelites were in bondage in Egypt for over 400 years and how they were beaten, starved, and treated as less than human.

"Now the sojourn of the children of Israel who lived in Egypt was four hundred and thirty years. And it came to pass at the end of the four hundred and thirty years—on that very same day—it came to pass that all the armies of the Lord went out from the land of Egypt" Exodus 12:40-41

I began to study not only the biblical text, but also historical texts and other religious text, including the Qur'an and some of the ancient texts that were said to have been removed from the original scrolls found containing different accounts of the Exodus and early ancient life. They were not adding up, and I became even angrier with my parents for raising me in this "religion" that seemed to point to the enslavement of our people. I thought they were hypocrites; therefore, I began to rebel. My dad was a strict disciplinarian, so even if I tried to debate with him in this area, or any area for that matter, I would have surely received discipline. So, I hid my research and studies outside of Christianity from them, until after I left home for the military.

Saul of Tarsus was a Roman soldier that was born into Jewish ancestry. He was a man that was taught the Hebrew scriptures yet is known throughout history as being the "man who persecuted Christians". As I began reading about his life, it was eerie how similar our lives were regarding being raised in religion (his Judaism and mine Christianity), both of us being a part of the national military, and how we both persecuted Christians. Now, I did not go as far as to imprison Believers in Christ, but I can certainly say I did in my heart. I say this with utmost humility and transparency. I wanted absolutely nothing to do with Christianity or the people that followed this *religion*.

"As for Saul, he made havoc of the church, entering every house, and dragging off men and women, committing them to prison" Acts 8:3

For almost ten years of my life, I not only found myself immersed in Islam and other religions and spiritual practices that celebrated people of color, but I also developed a strong dislike, of sorts, for those that did not look like me. I also found myself constantly debating my own mother, who was and yet is, a devout believer in Christ to the point, at times, of leaving her in tears. I regret putting her through this turmoil now, but I understand that it was a part of my own "Damascus Road Experience," as Saul had to be processed through, as well.

"As he journeyed he came near Damascus, and suddenly a light shone around him from heaven. Then he fell to the ground, and heard a voice saying to him, "Saul, Saul, why are you persecuting Me?" And he said, "Who are You, Lord?" Then the Lord said, "I am Jesus, whom you are persecuting. It is hard for you to kick against the goads." So he, trembling and astonished, said, "Lord, what do You want me to do?" Then the Lord said to him, "Arise and go into the city, and you will be told what you must do." And the men who journeyed with him stood speechless, hearing a voice but seeing no one. Then Saul arose from the ground, and when his eyes were opened he saw no one. But they led him by the hand and brought him into Damascus. And he was three days without sight, and neither ate nor drank" Acts 9:3-9.

Most followers of Islam, outside of the Arab world, choose to have their names changed due what they deem "erasing the white man's legacy" from their lineage and reclaiming their rightful ancestry. Yes, most slaves that were stolen from Africa had their names erased from their history and given the names of their slave masters. In this case, it was stripping them of their familial heritage and trying to erase any ties to where they originated. I did not like my name growing up: Christopher Lockwood Hunter, Jr. To me, it sounded like a "white man's name" and I wanted to erase all ties to it and take on a new name. Upon converting to Islam, I took on the name "Hakim" meaning *wise, revealing its bearer as a fountain of deep knowledge*. Knowledge was power to me, and at every turn, I sought knowledge of the history of people of color all over the world and even back into ancient times. I began to find out that my people were not always slaves and that many actually were the inventors of much of what we now enjoy in this country. I also realized that many were kings and queens in ancient history and were very wealthy and prosperous people in their native lands. Again, I became angry with this revelation.

Upon Saul's "Damascus Road Experience," God blinded his eyes for a period of three days in order to build his faith. During this time, he did not eat or drink. He was in a period of fasting and prayer. I also believe this is a type and shadow of Christ's death on the Cross and the symbolism of the three days before His resurrection. Somewhere along the line, Saul's name was changed to *Paul*. Whether this was initiated by God due to his new nature in Christ, or that it was simply another name he used is not known, but we are privy to God changing the names of the disciples due to their walking in their new nature. I, too, entered a season of *blindness* due to the loss of my first marriage. I was devastated and broken that my first wife left me and took our children from me. No matter what anyone says, divorce feels like death even to men. Though they may not want to admit this truth, it is, in fact, the truth. I was forced to go back home to my parents' house, so you can only imagine the chaos that was about to ensue now that I was officially practicing Islam. There was no peace in our home because I was constantly battling my mom about the evil of Christianity, and my dad threatening to kick me out if I did not respect his house.

Soon after, I moved out of my parents' house and lived house to house for a season. I was battling many demons during this time. I struggled with not having my children in my life and thought I was a failure as a father. I tried to restore my marriage, but it was not received and we did ultimately divorce. I was now out of the military for a season as I had served my first term honorably. I did not know what I was going to do, or where I was going. I was finally led to a church near my hometown and it was again, eerily similar to Saul's experience after he lost his sight on the Road to Damascus.

"Now there was a certain disciple at Damascus named Ananias; and to him the Lord said in a vision, "Ananias." And he said, "Here I am, Lord." So the Lord said to him, "Arise and go to the street called Straight, and inquire at the house of Judas for one called Saul of Tarsus, for behold, he is praying. And in a vision he has seen a man named Ananias coming in and putting his hand on him, so that he might receive his sight." Then Ananias answered, "Lord, I have heard from many about this man, how much harm he has done to Your saints in Jerusalem. And here he has authority from the chief priests to bind all who call on Your name." But the Lord said to him, "Go, for he is a chosen vessel of Mine to bear My name before Gentiles, kings, and the children of Israel. For I will show him how many things he must suffer for My name's sake." And Ananias went his way and entered the house; and laying his hands on him he said, "Brother Saul, the Lord Jesus, who appeared to you on the road as you came, has sent me that you may receive your sight and be filled with the Holy Spirit." Immediately there fell from his eyes something like scales, and he received his sight at once; and he arose and was baptized. So when he had received food, he was strengthened. Then Saul spent some days with the disciples at Damascus" Acts 9:10-19

My brokenness led me not only to a friend that brought me back to church, but also to the foot of the Cross where I denounced Islam and returned to the One true God of Heaven and Earth. The pastor of this church, God uses greatly to touch my heart, my soul, and my spirit. He knelt down with me and held me as I wept so deeply. He laid his hands on me and it was if my "eyesight was restored". Spiritual scales fell off of my eyes, and it was if a boulder was lifted off my chest. I, too, was filled with the Holy Spirit and I began to study the Word of God like I had never done so in my life. The truth was now coming to light and healing those dark and broken places in my life. Not long after, I met my new wife, *my true wife*, and God restored to me exactly what I had lost.

God had already been revealing Himself to me and showing me that Islam was not the absolute truth. But of course, due to my divorce, there was a lot of bitterness and anger within my heart. I struggled for years as God was slowly healing my heart and my mind. I still champion greatly my ethnicity and culture and fight for equality, even in the world of Christianity, where some still use the Gospel for their own selfish purposes and not the Way it was authentically birthed. Strangely enough, our God has a sense of humor. I married a woman outside of my ethnicity, though we do both share Native American ancestry. The very people I was harboring anger and, at times, hate for the atrocities committed against my people, God has joined me to in order to reveal not only His absolute love, but also His kindness and forgiveness.

Saul, now known as *Paul*, once hated Christians and abhorred what they stood for; upon his conversion, he became known as the greatest Apostle of all time. The things he once inflicted upon others, he was now suffering through for the cause of his Lord Jesus Christ, Yeshua the Messiah. What a true depiction of God's transformative power! God has allowed me the opportunity to serve 25 years in, and retire from, the military where I have traveled all around the world meeting people of all ethnicities, languages, backgrounds, and nations. It opened my eyes greatly to the vastness of God's Creation and His people all across the Earth.

I have developed long, lasting, and lifetime friendships with people from all walks of life and now share His truth with people from all kinds of religions and spiritual practices; yes, including Islam. I don't usurp superior knowledge and wisdom over these precious souls as if I have "arrived". No, God has given me not only a different spirit, but also His heart for people. He allowed me to go through the process in order to minister *firsthand* to others that have been blinded by religion. I can truly say, "I was once blind, and now I see!" John 9:25.

I encourage each of you reading this, there is a lost and dying world of people out there that simply do not know the truth. Many have been raised their entire lives in one religion or spiritual practice, generation after generation, and this is all they know. God is extending His own arm toward them, reaching them in their dreams, revealing Himself as the Way, the Truth, and the Life.

Many are turning their hearts to Him. Purpose to partner with Christ to reach them, not run them away through judgment. He loves them just like He loves you. Seek and pray that He gives you His heart for humanity, so we can all become laborers in His Great End Time Harvest! Paul chose the Way; I chose the Way. Will you choose that Way today and lay down your lives for Christ, so that many more can come to know His love and kindness?

Time is short and it is His desire that not one soul will perish!

Jacob

Frank Hernandez

"Afterward his brother came out, and his hand took hold of Esau's heel; so his name was called Jacob." Genesis 25:26

Have you ever felt alone, because of your life choices? You may have made mistake after mistake and now you are left alone with the voice of regret sounding loud in your heart. This is what the Bible says about Jacob who swindled, or tricked, his older brother Esau out of his rightful inheritance. Now, Jacob is about to meet up with his brother for the first time since it all happened.

"That night Jacob got up and took his two wives, his two female servants and his eleven sons and crossed the ford of the Jabbok. After he had sent them across the stream, he sent over all his possessions. So Jacob was left alone, and a man wrestled with him till daybreak" Genesis 32:22-24, NIV.

Like Jacob, I, too, was left alone in a prison cell because of my choices, where I came to a place of loneliness, and thoughts of regrets. My life was about to change in so many ways, though I did not know it yet. I was about to wrestle with the Lord. This was not a tag team match, or a group fight. It was a one-on-one fight where I was destined to lose yet gain so much more as a result of me losing. Looking back, as I read this portion of scripture, I wonder what Jacob was thinking at this moment, as he had wives, his sons, and all he possessed to go ahead of him? It was a time to either let regret take hold of his heart and end up feeling defeated, or allow his heart to be positioned to encounter the Presence of the Lord.

This is where so many people miss the voice, or leading, of the Holy Spirit. It is in the quiet, lonely place where the noise of life is silent, and the voice of the Lord becomes clear if we position our hearts towards Him. It was in a lonely, quiet jail cell that I heard the Lord ask me, "Will you stop now? Have you had enough son? I am here waiting for you to surrender." My eyes filled with tears as I know it was Him, yet even in that place, I was not ready to surrender. So, like Jacob, I began to wrestle with the Lord.

The fight was on. Instead of surrendering my heart and all that I am, I began to fight off the voice of the Holy Spirit. I actually had this idea that if I continued to live my life of sin and rebellion, the Lord would go away. I didn't want to hear His voice, so I began to do even more things that I felt would push Him away. I was wrong; He was wrestling with me, so the more I did what I wanted, the louder His voice became within me. It was a Holy conviction that I never felt before. However, eventually, I surrendered and gave my life to Jesus. It was a life changing moment for me. I had surrendered my life before, but this time was different. I knew that this was it. There was no going back. *"So Jacob was left alone, and a man wrestled with him till daybreak. When the man saw that he could not overpower him, he touched the socket of Jacob's hip so that his hip was wrenched as he wrestled with the man"* Genesis 32:24-25, NLT.

I had allowed the Lord to touch my life. In the scripture above, the Lord touches the socket of Jacob's hip. It caused him to walk with a limp. It was evident that Jacob was changed by this wrestling match because he walked differently after that fight. You see, after you surrender your life to the Lord, He will touch you in way that you will walk differently. For me, my limp was doing away with my gang mentality. Everything about my life had to change. Jesus had allowed my imprisonment as a tool to change me and strengthen my faith in Him. Let me explain.

I had begun a life being incarcerated since the age of twelve years old. I grew up with a lot of hurt and frustration. My biological father was not in my life, as he, too, was in out of prison. At the age of eight years old, my father was killed, so I wanted revenge. My only goal in life was to avenge his death. So, I began to get involved in street gangs here in Southern California. My life got chaotic, and I had grown cold hearted towards my family. The rest of my teenage life, I spent in numerous juvenile correctional facilities and spent time in prison as an adult, as well.

Being incarcerated presented another type of problem in my life; I grew to be very prejudice against black people because of the gang mindset in prisons. My gang culture was to hate blacks and those who associated with them. My young mind was full of hate and prejudice. So, when I gave my life to Christ, I had to really overcome the way I thought of others, In the gang culture, we never let anyone see us as weak. Scripture says that in our weakness, He is made strong. I had to learn to be weak, so that the strength of the Lord would become evident in my life. I fought and wrestled so much with the Holy Spirit.

"The man asked him, "What is your name?" "Jacob," he answered. Then the man said, "Your name will no longer be Jacob, but Israel, because you have struggled with God and with humans and have overcome" Genesis 32:27-28, NIV.

As I allowed my heart to change, I felt the Holy Spirit change me into a whole new man. I stopped hanging out with the old friends and crowds that I was all familiar with and most of all, that were familiar with the *old me*. I didn't realize it at first, but I just knew that I had to spend time serving in church. I had to be in the Word of God as much as I could. By the time I realized it, my life was changing. The Lord brought a spiritual father in my life that would drastically help catapult my life into what I am doing today. He was *black man* from Africa. You see, the Lord had to remove my prejudice and cold heart, so that this man could be the spiritual father that I needed in my life. When I finally surrendered and allowed the Lord touch my life, I changed and was able to embrace the plans He has had for me from the beginning of time.

"Jacob looked up and there was Esau, coming with his four hundred men; so he divided the children among Leah, Rachel and the two female servants. He put the female servants and their children in front, Leah and her children next, and Rachel and Joseph in the rear. He himself went on ahead and bowed down to the ground seven times as he approached his brother. But Esau ran to meet Jacob and embraced him; he threw his arms around his neck and kissed him. And they wept" Genesis 33:1-4, NIV.

It was unknown to Jacob what would happen as he faced his brother. It could be interpreted that he felt that Esau would take all that Jacob had since Jacob sent all he had ahead of him. You see, when you surrender all to the Lord, He restores all things. As you see in the scripture above, Esau embraced his brother. There are things in your life that are awaiting to embrace you. Things that you may fear, old enemies, old regrets, but as you surrender to the Lord, those things of old become a stepping stone instead of a stumbling block.

As you are reading this, has your heart been stirred? Maybe you have been feeling like the Lord has been calling you to the *more*, but you are so focused on how it should look that you have failed to see His plan because you are focused on your plan. Or maybe, the frustration of life has a hold on you. Your frustrated with the way things are going in your life, everything from work to relationships are failing. This is the Lord calling you out to your wrestling match; He really is looking for you to surrender it all to Him. Just as I did, in my loss, I gained everything in Him. Your walk in life will be different as you allow Him to touch you. As you let go of your old ways, He will impart His ways into your life. Never disregard the times you are alone. Just as Jacob had to face his past alone, the Lord met him and in that place, changed him and his name from Jacob to *Israel*.

I encourage you as you step out into the unknown where the Lord is waiting for you. May you let it all go and be changed in His presence.

Naaman

Kevin Michael Faulk

"And many lepers were in Israel in the time of Elisha the prophet, and none of them was cleansed except Naaman the Syrian." Daniel 1:6

Ll men desire that they would achieve great success in this life. Every man also expects that those successes would cause them to be revered by others. Is that not the ultimate human goal? Greatness to the degree that your name is praised long after you are dead? Naaman, the Captain of the Armies of the King of Syria, was such a man that wielded both achievement and renown in abundance.

"Now Naaman, captain of the host of the king of Syria, was a great man with his master, and honourable, because by him the LORD had given deliverance unto Syria: he was also a mighty man in valour..." 2 Kings 5:1.

*"Now Naaman, captain of the host of the king of Syria, was a great man with his master, and honourable, because by him the LORD had given deliverance unto Syria: he was also a mighty man in valour, **but he was a leper"*** 2 Kings 5:1.

Do you see the difference in the passage when I left out the five words that tarnish the apparent perfection of Naaman? How much did that omission/addition change the way you perceived him? Every man also has something to contend with that he did not choose, that which he would rather not come to the knowledge of others and honestly would prefer not to be aware of it himself: **weakness**. Be it defects of character, physical ailments, or mental sickness, most men despise and conceal that which negatively affects their lives, while either living in denial or attempting to eradicate it alone in silence. I know this because I have spoken to other men about it and I myself have attempted to hide my shortcomings and deep wounds from my past.

Even now, I find myself often attempting to save face rather than owning up to my failings and breaches of accountability. Why do I go through the exhausting routine of attempting to appear flawless when I know that I am not and am aware that everyone else is knowledgeable of that fact, as well? Well, that is because I want to be known by women, and by other men, as a great man. I want to be well-spoken of and well-received by all, celebrated even. I would love to be seen as an important, high-value man and treated as such by every person I meet. What man doesn't dream of such significance? For Naaman, that dream was a reality until he needed help with a problem that neither his prestige nor his military skills would be able to resolve.

"And the Syrians had gone out by companies, and had brought away captive out of the land of Israel a little maid; and she waited on Naaman's wife. And she said unto her mistress, Would God my Lord were with the prophet that is in Samaria! for he would recover him of his leprosy. And one went in, and told his Lord, saying, Thus and thus said the maid that is of the land of Israel. And the king of Syria said, Go to, go, and I will send a letter unto the king of Israel. And he departed, and took with him ten talents of silver, and six thousand pieces of gold, and ten changes of raiment. And he brought the letter to the king of Israel, saying, Now when this letter is come unto thee, behold, I have therewith sent Naaman my servant to thee, that thou mayest recover him of his leprosy" 2 Kings 5:2-6.

Picture it, the perfect setup for an epic narration of the ages, mighty Naaman travels to a foreign land bringing with him many great treasures with which to bestow upon the powerful prophet of a foreign God as a reward for releasing him from his horrid affliction. How grandiose and lofty Naaman would appear, even in his hour of desperate need! If only the Prophet had received the itinerary. Instead, Naaman arrived at his destination only to be met by the Prophet's assistant and was told that he would need to wash seven times in a nearby river in order to receive his healing. There was no royal welcome according to his status and no concern for the treasure he had brought with him. To say Naaman was disappointed would be an understatement.

"So Naaman came with his horses and with his chariot, and stood at the door of the house of Elisha. And Elisha sent a messenger unto him, saying, Go and wash in Jordan seven times, and thy flesh shall come again to thee, and thou shalt be clean. But Naaman was wroth, and went away, and said, Behold, I thought, He will surely come out to me, and stand, and call on the name of the LORD his God, and strike his hand over the place, and recover the leper. Are not Abana and Pharpar, rivers of Damascus, better than all the waters of Israel? may I not wash in them, and be clean? So he turned and went away in a rage" 2 Kings 5:9-12.

So, what was the problem with Naaman? That the solution to his incurable malady did not give him enough glory. His servant said it herself that he would have taken on a great task gladly if the Prophet had commanded it of him, but he was dejected because He was commanded instead to perform a simple task that anyone could've done. He never would have seen himself healed of his leprosy if he had held on to that pride. Though he was angry, he was shortly humbled to the point of obeying the words from the Prophet through his messenger. After washing seven times in the river that he audibly disdained, Naaman saw that his body was fully restored and rejoiced. At that moment, he learned that simple obedience to the Lord is greater than the lavish and dramatic showmanship of man. He so treasured the experience after the fact that he even decided that he wanted to take God back home with him.

"And Naaman said, Shall there not then, I pray thee, be given to thy servant two mules' burden of earth? for thy servant will henceforth offer neither burnt offering nor sacrifice unto other gods, but unto the LORD. In this thing the LORD pardon thy servant, that when my master goeth

into the house of Rimmon to worship there, and he leaneth on my hand, and I bow myself in the house of Rimmon: when I bow down myself in the house of Rimmon, the LORD pardon thy servant in this thing. And he said unto him, Go in peace. So he departed from him a little way" 2 Kings 5:17-19.

Naaman arrived to Elisha's house believing himself to be worthy of the service that he was prepared to pay the Prophet to perform; but before his return home, he identified himself as the servant of Elisha. What great humility was born in this commander of men that day! As a man, I want to know the correct way. I want to be the one who has every answer. I desire that all things were easy for me to accomplish and that I appeared as a champion even when in need. The simple truth of this is that those yearnings are idolatrous. I find myself often trying to become such a great man that I find myself to be praying that I may become God. Fortunately, He is gracious to bring that fact to my attention and to humble me in those seasons.

Like Naaman, I have had to learn that a great man is nothing compared to God, but a small man is such a one upon whom Jesus Christ can pour many blessings and work through to the praise of His mighty name.

Onesimus

Bill Faught, Jr.

"I appeal to you to show kindness to my child, Onesimus. I became his father in the faith while here in prison." Philemon 1:10, NLT

ach play has a backdrop and a script. Each story has a setting and a plot. The Apostle Paul's affectionate letters to the various churches is no different. While they vary a bit, each is an expression of love to the people of God from the man of God... and so it should be. Penned around 61 AD, Paul's one-chapter letter was written to Philemon, a church leader at Colossi defined as: *"divinely loved by God and a trusted worker in the ministry."* Also, the apostle lends his praise-worthy applause to fellow believers in this local expression of the Body of Christ for "walking in love" toward one another. He has received numerous reports about their pursuit of godly character and union illustrated, which became a great source of joy. Their gut-level compassion was commendable, too.

Interestingly enough, Philemon is the one epistle written to a man and not specifically to a congregated body of believers in Christ. The Epistle of Philemon is one of several letters written by Paul from his prison cell. Also, the opening text hints as if this letter was co-written by Timothy. This one-chapter book is just as important as the larger books of the New Testament, for it contains a very important element: walking in forgiveness with sisters and brothers in the Lord. This became one of the central themes of the Book of Philemon. The letter also has the themes of reconciliation. We shall not leave out neither of these all-important issues that are close to God's heart. They are the Lord's commands to all believers.

Some imprisoned believers would have been entirely preoccupied with worry and anxiety while being confined to a cell in the city of Rome, but it appears as if Paul takes full advantage of this "down-time" by reaching out to the dearest brothers and sisters attending the churches he planted throughout the years of his missionary journeys. The Apostle Paul illustrates the importance of "never resenting" the season believers find themselves in, at any given time. This is great advice coming from a prison cell. Don't you think?

As usual, the apostle of the Lord opens his letter to Philemon with greeting the saints, once again expressing his mushy heart. He is a genuine lover of both God and His global family. However, he is eager to get "right to the point". The Apostle Paul must have been in a "mode of restoration" to use such expressive words. The character in need of restoration is Onesimus, a new believer in Christ and a runaway slave. Starting with verse ten, the Apostle re-introduces the brother to the congregation. Earlier on, Onesimus was a member of the Church of Colossi, but long since remembered for being unprofitable and not beneficial to his former employer.

By this point in the story, though, Onesimus has been faithfully serving Paul, who was imprisoned in Rome. By now, the brother must have had a much different outlook on life, because the Apostle is quick to brag about his service to Paul "while in chains". Paul thought it was time to return Onesimus to the Church in Colossi, which presented a blessed opportunity to give and receive a good mix of forgiveness, reconciliation, and restoration from both parties. The Apostle thought the restoration of Onesimus was more important than remaining in Rome with him. Paul even states how easy it would have been to be selfish and hang on to him *like a ship tied to a dock,* but God had a much better, bigger plan.

The Apostle Paul recommends that the Church receive Onesimus with an upgrade: to move him from a servant to a brother for this is how the Apostle sees him, now. It was time to rejoin Onesimus with the community of believers in Colossi— it was time for this servant to show the fruit of his restoration. And Paul makes it abundantly clear, by saying, *"I will take care of"* whatever is owed. The Apostle's request included giving Onesimus "a fresh start". This is God's heart on display!

Verse ten, as taken from the original Greek text, gives a beautiful description of the transformation personally witnessed by the Apostle Paul in the life of Onesimus:

"Onesimus, my son in the Lord, has chosen the same way with you (Philemon): he chooses to remain up-close-and-personal, thus giving enough evidence to stand up in God's court of law that "a call to love" is the way. He was born again under my ministry; now, we share a fantastic father—son relationship in the Lord. By the way, this took place while I was in prison."

Paul's assurance of this former slave's transformation was such that he re-visits their past concerns, saying, *"There was a time when Onesimus failed to execute his duties, but he is no longer like that. He has become very profitable to me; indeed, I now believe he will also be to you"* [verse 11]. The Apostle is so convinced of this complete turn-around that he is willing to return Onesimus to demonstrate his gut-level compassion for their sake [verse 12].

Now, how's that for a transformed life and a biblical attempt to restore relationships? Deep down, Paul wanted to hold on to Onesimus for his own benefit, because he had served Paul over-the-top and above-and-beyond the call of duty while imprisoned in Rome. It seems as if Onesimus was sent as a billboard of God's love and grace, saying, *"Now, you will understand just how beneficial he really is"* [verse 13].

After the Church in Colossi had given their consent [verse 14], the Apostle gives one contingency that would display restoration on their side, saying, *"...I am hoping that you keep him the rest of his life"* [verse 15] . And if that wasn't enough, Paul adds a weight to his expectations for absolute restoration requiring: *"...but no more a slave, without any ownership rights of his own. Now, receive him as one loved by God and a member of His family. This how I see Onesimus; and, this is how I have been treating him. Now, I know you feel the same and even more so, seeing him as both your fellow man and your brother in the Lord, the one who exercises absolute ownership rights as Master and Lord"* [verse 16].

The Church in Colossi had long since taken the Apostle into their community of believers. Now, he is asking for them to strongly take a personal interest in Onesimus like they did him. Beloved, restoration is a slippery slope. Often, if people allow the one in need of restoration back into church, they must enter through the back door. They will be watched like a hawk, as the expression goes. Phrases like, "I trust you, but..." are the most popular. Yet, Paul does not select such language. He's requiring more—a better way. The Apostle takes one final "leap of faith" in the restoration of this brother "fallen-from-grace". Much like the Good Samaritan, who paid for the care of the injured man, Paul offers to "take care" of all past and future indebtedness owed by Onesimus. In fact, the Apostle Paul clearly states his intentions, saying,

"I don't want Onesimus to owe anything to anyone as he makes this fresh start—laying to rest any perceived indebtedness on your part" [verse 18-19].

Indeed, Paul's attempt to put any argument against Onesimus to rest is commendable, asking the Body of Christ to make every effort to do above-and-beyond what was written in his letter to Philemon [verse 22]. Any attempt to restore "such a one" without a spirit of meekness will resemble a sludge pit at a waste plant, instead of a great moment for celebration. Christ-honoring meekness will steer a believer away from legalism [Galatians 6:1].

I was Onesimus for a season, but in a different way. As a teenager, I struggled with "not wanting to be different". I knew there was a call to ministry from age twelve, but being popular in school was a speed bump not so easily maneuvered. Spiritually, everything came to a halt. I was cold and indifferent to God. In my own way, I was unprofitable. My father was thousands of miles away serving in Vietnam and my mother was mentally struggling to balance life and raise five kids on her own. By the grace of God, mother called on a pastor friend who willingly drove four hours one way to with visit me. Upon his arrival, I shall never forget Brother Taylor immediately striking up a conversation with me about the condition of my heart before the Lord. And he fought for me! Through embattled prayer, he pulled me out of the horrible spiritual pit in which I was drowning. Also, at that moment, I felt honored and made to feel important as Brother Taylor spent an entire Saturday between driving and praying for me.

There is nothing more affirming than knowing one is willing to get into the trenches with those who are struggling to find their way to Jesus. Kicking people to the spiritual curb is so NOT like God, but it seems to be the current trend in some church circles. Restoration and forgiveness is a muddy process through which many are unwilling to go. Yet, if Jesus is willing to leave the ninety-nine to rescue the one, so should we.

There is much to learn from this one-chapter letter to Philemon. We only see the tip of the iceberg, but now that you and I have caught a "whiff" of what is being "cooked up" in God's kitchen, consider hanging out to catch the entire meal by reading the Book of Philemon.

Beloved, stay poised to love and restore others. I'll see you there!

Mordecai

E. Lawrence Williams

"In Shushan the citadel there was a certain Jew whose
name was Mordecai the son of Jair, the son of Shimei, the son of Kish, a
Benjamite." Esther 2:5

I n some books of the Bible, there are many anonymous characters and God becomes the main focus of Scripture. In one book in particular, God's name is never mentioned, yet to the discerning spirit, His actions are very prevalent. In the Book of Esther, there are characters of great significance mentioned, but the invisible hand of God is even more predominant in the affairs of men. Three of the powerfully prominent and contrasted figures in the Book of Esther are Mordecai, Haman, and Xerxes.

Mordecai is a solid nonconformist, while Haman represented the arrogant and ruthless minister of state; Xerxes ruled his subjects as an authoritarian and reckless king. Yet, as visible as these three are, behind them is an unseen and unnamed Presence—the God of Israel protecting His exiled people. Xerxes honored Haman by promoting him and giving him authority over all of the princes who were with him and all of the king's servants bowed down and paid homage to Haman by command of the king, Esther 3:1-2. That is, everyone except Mordecai.

While the throng of servants lay flat on their faces as Haman pranced by, Mordecai stood up erect because he was not going to bend the knee to anyone except Jehovah. If he had wanted to do so, he probably could have dialed up a plausible excuse to prostrate himself before the second most powerful man in the kingdom and compromise his spirit—but he didn't! Mordecai worshipped the only true God, Jehovah, which was too deeply engrained within him to bow to a mortal, so he maintained a stiff backbone and refused to bow. What a courageous act in the face of evil! Anyone who knew that he was a Jew would understand why he didn't follow the crowd. However, his obstinate behavior further isolated him and those who observed his act of refusing to bow reported it to the authorities.

There are those times when we have to associate with people in a work relationship where our faith in Christ is not shared. Co-workers will discover our reluctance to do things that will dishonor Christ and the word goes out that we are described as "nonconformist" and straight-laced. Unfortunately, the hardest thing for some Christians to do is to disregard the persistent solicitations of others and stay ready to be singular minded. We need to avoid any risk of complying with the world's demands. Wisdom for the Christian is to fiercely resist the world because of our fear of God.

Proverbs 1:7 tells us, *"The fear of the LORD is the beginning of knowledge; Fools despise wisdom and instruction."*

It seemed Mordecai was more diplomatic than religious, but he impressively enforced his assurance that Israel could not perish, because he believed that Providence placed people in their respective places for great, unselfish ends. He believed that Esther had been installed as Queen to influence Xerxes to save the Jews from Haman's Satanic plot. Mordecai believed that he also was put in place to be an influencer to Queen Esther when he overheard a plot to kill the king, Xerxes. He reported the plot to Queen Esther and she relayed it to the King; the two men were hanged and the incident was recorded in the royal archives. Mordecai was a watchman.

So, what was the connection between Mordecai and Queen Esther? Esther 2:20 gives us the answer:

"Esther had not yet made known her kindred or her people, even as Mordecai had commanded her; for Esther did what Mordecai told her as she had done when under his care."

Mordecai had raised, as his own daughter, an orphaned cousin named *Hadassah*, later known as Esther. He may have been a eunuch because there is no mention of a wife or children and when Esther was chosen to be in the harem, he regularly checked on her, Esther 2:11. Mordecai was a responsible and protective guardian. It is very much like Jews to keep the relationship between Mordecai and Esther a secret. Perhaps, nobody knew that Mordecai was the queen's cousin with the exception of one, maybe two trusted servants. Mordecai was a man in stealth.

But as we move forward, we see in chapter three Haman has made a false and malicious representation of the Jews, and their character and Xerxes buys into it. Haman considered the Jews to be highly dangerous because they had their own laws and did not conform to the statutes of the Persian Kingdom. Therefore, they were viewed as a disaffected people worthy of extinction before they could infect others with their regulation, which could end up in a rebellion. We not only see God's invisible hand in the Book of Esther, but we can also clearly see Satan's volcanic activity, as well. Haman bids very high to exterminate the Jews (3:9) because he knew there were many people in the provinces that hated the Jews and would gladly kill them for a reward. In still yet another unfortunate moment, King Xerxes bought into the proposal because he was so bewitched by Haman and his assertions.

Mordecai had made a strong impression upon Esther earlier to do what she was born to do, and that was to see the King and expose Haman for the pile of dung he was born to be. She made a bold approach to the King with one maid holding the train of her dress and another maid holding her up as she approached Xerxes. She came to the King in radiance of spirit, a cheerful face, but a heart filled with sorrow because of Haman's plot against her people. When the King summoned her into the throne room, he asked her what she wished, and she invited the King and Haman to a banquet at her quarters. The King called for Haman, and they attended the banquet and drank wine. The King again asked Esther what her wish was and by Providence, she invited them to come back the next day, which was a delay in what she wanted to tell the King.

After the Queen's invite, Haman headed for home to brag to his family and friends about being invited, along with the King, to dine at the Queen's quarters. But as his happy heart went through the gate, guess who he encountered? Mordecai was at the gate and was as determined as ever. He did not stand up or even move for Haman. Mordecai acted so from a principle of conscience in which he persevered without cringing to Haman, and Mordecai had no regret. Especially when he had reason to fear Haman because Mordecai knew that God could and would deliver him and his people from the rage of Haman. This was also an opportunity for God to solidify the faith of Mordecai and grow the faith of Esther. This is something that I have had to be aware of in my own walk with Christ.

Ephesians 2:8-9 says, *"For by grace you have been saved through faith; and that not of yourselves, it is the gift of God; not as a result of works, so that no one may boast."*

This means that the faith I have is given to me by God and He determined to give me the gift of faith before He laid the foundation of the world. Since the faith that I have belongs to Him, only He can grow it at the times He has predetermined. Faith does not necessarily grow in times of peace and prosperity, but in times of varying degrees of adversity tempered by God's love, grace, and mercy. God owns my faith, and He alone grows it!

Mordecai's disrespect of Haman took the sap out of his happiness, and he was angrier than ever because this little affront, which he received from Mordecai, was the dead fly that spoiled his precious ointment of pride. Solomon said a couple of things about prideful people like Haman.

Proverbs 21:24 says, *"Proud," "Haughty," "Scoffer," are his names, Who acts with insolent pride."*

How about Proverbs 16:18?

"Pride goes before destruction, And a haughty spirit before stumbling."

The obedient life of a Christian is the dead fly in the precious ointment of the world we live in and for that reason, the world hates Christians. The worldly citizen hates our lives because the Light we have in us exposes their nakedness and filth and so as a result, our lives are a stench to their nostrils.

"To the one we are an aroma that brings death; to the other, an aroma that brings life. And who is equal to such a task?" 2 Corinthians 2:16.

Aristotle wrote, "Vultures are killed with oil of roses."

Pliny said, "Swine cannot live in some parts of Arabia by reason of the sweet scent of aromatic trees growing there and tigers are enraged with perfumes."

Haman rendered Mordecai as a stench in his nostrils and his meditation was revenge.

There came a night when the King could not sleep, Esther 6:1. The truth is that God was at work, and He would not let Xerxes sleep because it was time to recall and reward. Sleep is a gift from God, and He can break it anytime He desires. I have had those times when I fell asleep, woke up, and could not get back to sleep no matter how many puppies I counted. It is in these times that God interrupts our sleep and is calling us to get up, read His Word, and pray. Confess our sin or to just be still and quiet for a moment or two. It also may be a time of recall or revelation. God owns sleep! The King ordered to have the book of records, the journal of his reign, read to him, and Mordecai's deed was read. Xerxes, being wide awake, did not call for wine, women, or music, but called for what God put into his heart. The King read the incident concerning two of the King's eunuchs who were bent on assassinating him. When he noted that the plot was reported by Mordecai, he quickly determined to honor him. Was it Mordecai's plan to be at the exact spot where he could listen to the plot against the King? Probably not, because he may have wanted to be somewhere else. But it was by Providence that he was in a place to overhear the plans of the two eunuchs.

Solomon says in Proverbs 16:9, *"The mind of man plans his way, But the LORD directs his steps."*

Mordecai was always exactly where God wanted him and the same is true for us. From this, we can see Xerxes had no clue that God spared his life by appointing Mordecai to be in the right place at the right time. Most of the world does not realize that God has strategically placed the Christian in this world for the benefit of it. Mordecai was a strategic benefit and a blessing to Xerxes. But we must remember that God was in complete control of the circumstances, because He designed them. For what purpose? It was for the good of His people and the same is true for us today.

Paul said in Romans 8:28, *"And we know that God causes all things to work together for good to those who love God, to those who are called according to His purpose."*

Persia was not the home of Mordecai and the Jews, and this world is not the home of the Christian. God had a purpose for Mordecai and without him, Haman would have successfully carried out his Satanic scheme. God has us here to carry out His will by calling out His elect using the Gospel message. Also, we must remember that God is still fulfilling His promise to Abraham when he said,

"Go forth from your country, And from your relatives And from your father's house, To the land which I will show you; And I will make you a great nation, And I will bless you, And make your name great; And so you shall be a blessing; And I will bless those who bless you, And the one who curses you I will curse. And in you all the families of the earth will be blessed" Genesis 12:1-3.

Again, I say God has strategically placed us in this world to be a blessing to others and because we are Spirit-filled, some will embrace God and receive special blessings, while others will reject Him and receive common grace. Those who settle for God's common grace until their earthly life is over, will be in the deadliest danger of receiving the eternal punishment of Judas and Haman.

Heavenly Father, thank You for allowing us to participate in the work You are doing in this world. Also, Father, thank You for directing our steps and strategically placing Your children in this world to bless others in our service to Your Son, Jesus Christ! Amen!

Jephthah

Elijah Valley

"And Jephthah made a vow to the LORD, and said, "If You will indeed deliver the people of Ammon into my hands, then it will be that whatever comes out of the doors of my house to meet me, when I return in peace from the people of Ammon, shall surely be the LORD'S, and I will offer it up as a burnt offering." Judges 11:30-31

I have had the Kingdom privilege of traveling on missionary journeys to the East African Nation of Uganda. This beautiful nation, also known as "The Pearl of Africa," is filled with "Believers" who love Jesus. Each journey has been filled with wonderful experiences. Worship services are exciting from start to finish. There are plenty of places to eat great food. Most people are extremely nice! The main downside of visiting Uganda is the traffic jams in Kampala. Kampala, the capital city, has grown from 95,000 in 1950 to about 4 million people in 2023. "Jams," as they call them, are unpredictable! While there are highway codes, traffic laws, and even driving schools, none of these matter in a "jam!" Two lanes become four lanes. These "jams" are filled with thousands of 14 passenger Toyota vans, taxis, and "Boda, bodas," their version of motorcycle taxis.

On my last trip to Uganda, as we were running short on time to get to the airport, our prayer was: "Lord, please do not let there be any "jams!" During that trip, two men who are known for being prompt called me to tell me they were "stuck in a jam." When anyone else is scheduled to pick me up, I stay in my room until the front desk calls to tell me they have arrived. For these two men, I go to the lobby just before scheduled pick up time because they are prompt. When they called to say they were "stuck in a jam," I knew it was beyond their control. I have lived long enough to know life can be filled with "jams." Some "jams" are predictable; others are unpredictable. Some "jams" are of our own making, while others are beyond our control. At some point, most of us have cried, "Lord, if you get me out of this…" or "Lord, if you fix this for me…"

In Judges 11, the Children of Israel are stuck in a jam. This jam was of their own making because of their disobedience. In four separate verses, the writer of Judges summarized their disobedience: *"In those days there was no king in Israel; everyone did what was right in his own eyes."* This indicates they had a leadership crisis! They were "stuck in a jam," because they lacked real leadership. After Joshua's death, there was no constant leader in Israel. God raised up eight individuals as "judges" to deliver Israel from an enemy. These judges could be compared to New Testament Apostles. By the time we reach this 11th chapter, The Lord had run out of patience with Israel. They were in the constant sin, repent, sin, repent cycle.

"So the Lord said to the children of Israel, "Did I not deliver you from the Egyptians and from the Amorites and from the people of Ammon and from the Philistines? Also the Sidonians and Amalekites and Maonites oppressed you; and you cried out to Me, and I delivered you from their hand. Yet you have forsaken Me and served other gods. Therefore I will deliver you no more. Go and cry out to the gods which you have chosen; let them deliver you in your time of distress" Judges 10:11–14, NKJV.

In other words, "didn't I deliver you seven times before, or from seven different nations?" Seven is the biblical number of completion, or perfection. The Lord was tired of their empty repentance. After studying my Bible for a while, I have seen a number of patterns. One such pattern is how God dealt with disobedience in the Old Testament. In the Old Testament, God used an enemy to whip Israel back into place and then punished the enemy for having the nerve to touch God's children. In Judges 11, it was the Sons of Ammon. After another lukewarm repentance of Israel, God raised up an uncommon warrior to deliver His people. Here, we meet Jephthah. Jephthah was not your typical leader. He was not born of a virgin; he was born of a harlot. Like Joseph, his brothers despised him. So much so, they kicked him out of their father's house. These half-brothers declared Jephthah would not receive any of their father's inheritance. Jephthah fled to the land of Tob where he was joined by a band of "worthless fellows". The Complete Jewish Bible says, *"He enlisted a gang of rowdies who would go out raiding with him."*

Of their own makings, Israel is stuck in another "jam." Scholars consider this "jam" as the sixth apostasy in the Book of Judges. Six, in your Bible, is the number of man. The men of Israel swallowed their pride and recruited Jephthah as their captain. Jephthah pushed back saying, *"Did you not hate me and drive me out of my father's house? Why have you come to me now when you are in distress?"* As the cliche goes, they were desperate men calling for desperate measures. A wise man said, *"Pride goes before destruction, And a haughty spirit before a fall"* Proverbs 16:18, NKJV. They were stuck in a jam! After accepting the leadership post, Jephthah makes a hasty "Lord, if you help me" vow.

"If You will indeed deliver the people of Ammon into my hands, then it will be that whatever comes out of the doors of my house to meet me, when I return in peace from the people of Ammon, shall surely be the LORD'S, and I will offer it up as a burnt offering."

The beginning of verse 29 was all Jephthah needed. It says, *"Then the Spirit of the LORD came upon Jephthah..."* Jephthah had everything he needed before he made this reckless vow. His reckless vow demonstrated a lack of understanding of the anointing on his life as well as the Mosaic law. Under the Mosaic law, people could not be used for burnt offerings. In the Old Testament, the Spirit came upon certain people at certain times and empowered them to accomplish God's purpose. With the anointing on his life, Jephthah smote and subdued 20 cities within about a 40-mile radius.

"So Jephthah crossed over to the Ammonites to fight against them, and the Lord gave them into his hand. And he struck them from Aroer to the neighborhood of Minnith, twenty cities, and as far as Abel-keramim, with a great blow. So the Ammonites were subdued before the people of Israel" Judges 11:32–33, ESV.

I wonder who, or what, Jephthah thought would be the first to come out of his door when he returned. During that time, it was customary for women to come out to meet a victorious army and celebrate with dancing and tambourines. This is why Jephthah's daughter, his only child, was the first person to come out of his house when he returned from the war. I wonder what would have happened if Jephthah reneged on his vow. He was certainly "stuck in a jam." This one of his own making.

The Bible says he tore his clothes, which is a symbol of repenting, or sorrow. "I have given my word to the Lord, and I cannot go back on it." Leviticus 27 says you must fulfill your vows to The LORD. Talk about being "stuck in a jam!" Clearly, the big idea in this story is whenever you are "stuck in a jam," do not make rash, or reckless, vows. Jephthah live about 200 years before David was born. In Psalm 141:3, King David wrote,

"Set a guard, O LORD, over my mouth; Keep watch over the door of my lips." The original text reads, *"Station O Yahweh a guard for my mouth, keep watch over the door of my lips."*

The word "station" reminds me of military people who are stationed around the world. They have been strategically sent to those locations to defend America's interests.

In 1 Corinthians 13:11, the Apostle Paul wrote, *"When I was a child, I spoke as a child, I understood as a child, I thought as a child; but when I became a man, I put away childish things."*

"When I became a man" speaks of maturity. One of the main indicators of maturity is knowing the right time to speak and the right words when you speak.

"To everything there is a season, A time for every purpose under heaven" Ecclesiastes 3:1, NKJV.

"A time to tear, And a time to sew; A time to keep silence, And a time to speak;" Ecclesiastes 3:7, NKJV.

The next time you find yourself "stuck in a jam," drop the "LORD, if You..." prayer and walk by faith. Trust the anointing on your life and navigate your way through the "jam." Like Google Maps or the Waze app, use the Word of God as your GPS. However, you have to listen to the voice of Holy Spirit as He guides you into all truth. If you take a shortcut, or the wrong turn, you may end up stuck in a different jam. By faith we understand, God will work this jam out for the good.

Let me close with a short testimony. I got saved when I was ten years old. When I left home as a 19-year-old, I put my faith on a shelf. For about four years, I did almost "everything I was big enough and bad enough to do." I probably went to four worship services in four years. That life got me stuck in a couple "jams". During each "jam," I made a "LORD, if You help me" vow. Finally, as my family and I were relocating to the USA, I remember perhaps my last "LORD, if You help me" vow. While flying over the Atlantic Ocean, my fear of flying got the best of me. I stated: "Lord, if You help me, I will get back in church." I am proud to say, I have done a pretty good job keeping this vow. I also learned it is the fear of dying, not the fear of flying.

While I am still under God's construction, I am learning to live a life that does not keep me stuck in one jam after another. I pray the LORD will grace you with the same power!

Nehemiah

Baxter Stanley

"The words of Nehemiah the son of Hachaliah. It came to pass in the month
of Chislev, in the twentieth year, as I was in Shushan the citadel."
Nehemiah 1:1

The first three chapters of Nehemiah introduce us to Nehemiah. When we meet him, he is serving as the cup bearer to Artaxerxes, King of Persia. This job was more than just bringing beverages to the King; Nehemiah had to taste everything before giving it to the King. If Nehemiah didn't die from poisoning, the beverage would then be served to the King. What an insight concerning Nehemiah! He was no stranger to risking his life for his boss. In fact, that was his very job description!

Nehemiah was the son of Jews who were captured and taken from Jerusalem to Babylon. By the time we meet him, the seventy years of captivity prescribed by God had been completed. The Jews had been given permission from Cyrus to return to Jerusalem, and two groups had already gone home and begun work on rebuilding the Temple. Our interest in his story concerns how Nehemiah's life was intersected by a problem that others had already been assigned to deal with and his transition from serving a foreign king to serving the God of his people and the people of his God.

Nehemiah Chapter 1:

"These are the memoirs of Nehemiah son of Hacaliah. Nehemiah's Concern for Jerusalem. In late autumn, in the month of Kislev, in the twentieth year of King Artaxerxes' reign, I was at the fortress of Susa. Hanani, one of my brothers, came to visit me with some other men who had just arrived from Judah. I asked them about the Jews who had returned there from captivity and about how things were going in Jerusalem. They said to me, "Things are not going well for those who returned to the province of Judah. They are in great trouble and disgrace. The wall of Jerusalem has been torn down, and the gates have been destroyed by fire. "When I heard this, I sat down and wept. IN FACT, FOR DAYS I MOURNED, FASTED, AND PRAYED TO THE GOD OF HEAVEN."

Around December of 446 B.C., Nehemiah reports that a brother of his and some friends came to visit him in Susa. These men had just come from Judah. Nehemiah asks them how things are in Jerusalem, and they give him a very dismal report. We learn a lot about Nehemiah by the way this negative report affects him. Chapter one, verse four, tells us that Nehemiah sat down and began to weep! He mourned, fasted, and prayed for several days to the God of Heaven. We don't know exactly how long this went on, but the next date referenced was April, or May, of the next year. That's what we call a high-impact report!

We can learn a lot from the way Nehemiah prayed. *"... FOR DAYS I MOURNED, FASTED, AND PRAYED TO THE GOD OF HEAVEN. Then I said, "O LORD, God of heaven, the great and awesome God who keeps his covenant of unfailing love with those who love him and obey his commands, listen to my prayer! Look down and see me praying night and day for your people Israel. I confess that we have sinned against you. Yes, even my own family and I have sinned! We have sinned terribly by not obeying the commands, decrees, and regulations that you gave us through your servant Moses."*

The first step was mourning, followed by fasting and praying to God. This took some time, but Nehemiah wasn't experiencing a knee-jerk reaction that would leave as quickly as it arrived. The next step was **repentance**! This is no longer a popular or oft-practiced activity for many people. Nehemiah repented for himself, his family, and his people. It takes humility to assume the responsibility for sins you didn't even commit, but we will see God honor Nehemiah for doing it.

I'm sixty-seven years old. I've been in church all my life, and I've seen a lot of stuff. The old saints at my mom's church would say that Nehemiah received a **burden** from the Lord. While we don't hear much about that anymore, the concept of receiving a burden needs to make a comeback!

In Matthew, Jesus says: *Come to Me, all you who labor and are heavy laden, and I will give you rest. Take My yoke upon you and learn from Me, for I am gentle and lowly in heart, and you will find rest for your souls. For My yoke is easy and My burden is light."*

It would be wrong to conclude that Jesus was discouraging us from taking on challenges that require hard work and just "lean on the everlasting arm!" Instead, He was saying that we should trade the mundane, wearisome tasks of self-serving lifestyles for the burden that He places on us. Even though the burden that Nehemiah comprehended and accepted caused him an initial "breakdown" of sorts, his immediate approach to God for help and favor opened the door to all the resources that he would need to accomplish the task before him.

The following Spring, after much prayer and fasting, Nehemiah gets his opportunity to approach Artaxerxes for permission to go to Jerusalem and intervene on behalf of his homeland. The concept of a weighty burden may be perceived by some as a lack of favor from the Lord, or "walking beneath the privilege" of a Believer. However, it was the weighty burden that caused the sad countenance on Nehemiah's face when he served Artaxerxes that Spring. The King had never seen Nehemiah sad before, so he initiated the conversation about what was bothering Nehemiah. Artaxerxes was perceptive, recognizing the difference between a physical illness and an emotional crisis. Essentially, he just asked Nehemiah, "What's up with you, man?" It's noteworthy that Nehemiah didn't have to ask the King, the King asked Nehemiah!

Nehemiah's reply was, *"Long live the king! How can I not be sad? For the city where my ancestors are buried is in ruins, and the gates have been destroyed by fire."* His answer was direct and to the point. He didn't make it about Nehemiah, he made it about Jerusalem. It wasn't expressed as a concern for the object of his need, but as the object of need of the place His God loved! The King's immediate response was *"Well, how can I help you?"* What's the difference in focusing on our needs and focusing on what concerns God? In a word, **RESULTS!**

There is a huge lesson to be learned from Nehemiah at this point of the story: When the one who had the authority and resources to supply everything that Nehemiah needed to accomplish his mission asks how he can help, Nehemiah already has a ready answer! There was no "let me get back to you" coming across Nehemiah's lips. It's obvious that his days/months of praying and fasting were not just whining sessions before God, but rather a deeply probing consultation and assessment of the situation and what it would take to get Jerusalem properly sorted.

"When I came to the governors of the province west of the Euphrates River, I delivered the king's letters to them. The king, I should add, had sent along army officers and horsemen to protect me. [10] But when Sanballat the Horonite and Tobiah the Ammonite official heard of my arrival, they were very displeased that someone had come to help the people of Israel" Nehemiah 2:9

With the King's blessing, Nehemiah sets out for Jerusalem armed with letters from Artaxerxes to various officials instructing them to give safe passage and supplies for Nehemiah and his group. From the moment of his arrival, there were those who opposed his presence and his mission to help the people of Jerusalem. It would be easy to get distracted by the fact that Nehemiah's physical mission was to rebuild the wall and overlook the fact that it was the poor condition of his people that caused him to mourn, pray, fast, and undertake the burden in the first place.

Whenever God's people are in a bad situation, someone is always benefiting from their misery. Those people are never glad to hear of the impending improvement of God's people, or the deliverance of God's people, from their extortion of them. One of the most valuable lessons we can learn from Nehemiah's exemplary leadership is his constant focus on the mission and his refusal to give time to his detractors.

Three days after arriving in Jerusalem, Nehemiah surveys the condition of the walls of Jerusalem at night. We've heard the old saying, "Loose lips sink ships". Nehemiah understood this principle and kept his cards close to his chest. He was already aware that he had opposition and knew that giving them information would enable them to use that to work against him. We have a better chance for success when God is our audience more than and before the public. Nehemiah conducted his assessment under the cover of night to avoid distracting encounters with his opposition.

In a social media dominated culture, we could benefit greatly by learning to avoid distractions as we seek to accomplish the mission of God. We can't demand that people attend all-night prayer meetings to solve all of our problems, but we can accomplish much more if we can master the art of disconnecting from the internet long enough to pray like Nehemiah prayed and optimize our action plans by avoiding need-less interruptions. Once Nehemiah finished his survey, he addressed the people and cast his vision, Nehemiah 2:16. Sanballat and Tobiah imme-diately ratchet up their opposition, but Nehemiah just puts them in their place by restating the mission and informing them that they have no part in it!

Chapter three gives the details of the assignments given to the people to build the wall. The details are valuable, but we will concern ourselves with the bigger picture. Nehemiah knew the value and necessity of a leader delegating responsibility and resources to the people. Listen to Nehemiah's words at the end of verse 18: "*They began the good work!*" Nehemiah shouldered the burden for rebuilding the wall, but he never saw it as a solo act. He knew that teamwork makes the dream work! Nehemiah aligned the various tasks with the people whose strengths were best suited to those tasks.

When leaders lead by allowing people to use their gifts appropriate-ly, the mission at hand has its best chance of success. Servant leadership is not about doing the work for the people; rather, releasing people to do their best at utilizing their God-given gifts.

In Nehemiah chapter four, we are reminded that everybody being on task and the mission moving forward doesn't make everybody happy. In fact, we read that when Sanballat saw the work progressing, it angered him and he flew into a rage! His buddy, Tobiah, joined him in taunting the Jews and threatening to do them harm. These are typical behaviors of small minded, insecure people. They threatened to report Nehemiah and his followers as rebels who opposed the King. Not a great strategy since Nehemiah never moved a rock before getting the approval of the King. Nevertheless, Sanballat and Tobiah appealed to their cronies and planned to gather a large army to attack Jerusalem and throw Nehemiah and the entire city into confusion.

The devil's favorite strategy against the saints is isolation and confusion. If he can make confusion the order of the day, he has no need to kill him. He'd rather have us alive and confused than dead and quiet. Nehemiah's first defense was prayer, Nehemiah 4:4. We see that continued prayer led to continued progress.

The next verses reveal that Nehemiah didn't just delegate work, he included the people in the prayer battle! *"But **we prayed to our God** and guarded the city day and night to protect ourselves.* The power of corporate prayer cannot be overstated, nor can the necessity to be diligent in setting watch against the enemy of our souls. Our walk with God is not just a walk in the park. We have an enemy who hates us, whose mission is to steal, kill, and destroy. I'm glad Jesus came that we might have life, more abundantly!

The next obstacle Nehemiah faced was not just the enemy coalition that had formed against him. It may still be one of the most difficult things for churches and Christian groups to overcome, today. We're talking about **volunteer fatigue**! Even though they were praying as they worked, at about the halfway mark, the people began to complain.

As leaders, it's easy to just focus on the fact that the people are complaining and resent them for it. We need to focus instead on the cause of the complaining. Fatigue is not the fruit of being an evil person, certainly not a lazy person. People who work hard in the face of adversity are still vulnerable to fatigue. We don't need to lecture them, we need to encourage them. We need to remind them of the success they've already achieved and point them to God, our source of strength and victory, and toward the finish line that is just ahead.

That's exactly how Nehemiah handled it, Nehemiah 4:10-23. Nehemiah listened to the people, then pointed them toward the God they were serving and to their loved ones who would benefit from their success. Simply put, he called them to remember and fight for their families!

In chapter six, we see that the wall is completed, despite the opposition. Sanballat and Tobiah continued to harass and threaten Nehemiah and the people of Jerusalem, and Nehemiah continued to refuse to pay them any attention. At one point, when they demanded a meeting with him, Nehemiah responded by saying words to the effect of "Why should I stop my important work to come talk with you?" More work and less talk is often a good idea!

After the wall and gates were completed, Nehemiah addressed the spiritual need of the people by having Ezra read the Word in the presence of all the people. They made commitments to honor God and the Temple. They promised to treat each other rightly and to not chase after other gods. After attending to these matters, Nehemiah returned to Susa as he had promised Artaxerxes. In his absence, the people allowed Tobiah to set up a room for himself in the Temple of the Lord. Nehemiah returns to find this incredible reality and deals with it swiftly and strongly. From this we learn that diligence must be given to maintain what God has enabled us to accomplish and never make place for the enemy to occupy what has been built for God with the help of God.

The story of Nehemiah is one of the greatest resources on leadership ever written. It has been used to teach leadership in the military as well as in Christian schools and colleges. While we haven't dealt with every issue presented in the Book of Nehemiah, there are some outstanding principles that we have observed. The first is the fact that there is no record of God ever saying to Nehemiah, "Thou shalt go to Jerusalem and rebuild the walls!" God spoke to Noah and told him to build an ark, Genesis 6:13-15. Moses heard God speak from a burning bush, Genesis 3:1-4:14. Nehemiah just heard a bad report from his brother who had just returned from Jerusalem that broke his heart and drove him to pray and ask God to help him do something about it.

Tommy Barnett, Pastor Emeritus of Phoenix First Assembly says, "Find a need and fill it" when asked how churches should do ministry. There's no lack of things that need to be done, and God will provide what is needed to do the job when anyone catches the vision of, and burden for, the task. We're not saying Nehemiah wasn't called, just that he never heard an incredibly large voice saying, "Go, do this or that."

The next leadership principle we see from Nehemiah is that of spending time praying and fasting before launching any plans. Remember, it wasn't minutes or hours, but days and weeks that Nehemiah spent praying. Ultimately, he spent time repenting for himself and others before he petitioned God for what he needed to accomplish his mission. Nehemiah didn't see the favor of God as some special treatment for himself, but as the provision by God of what he needed to do the work of God.

The focus and strategic thinking of Nehemiah needs to be imitated by all who seek to lead. How many times have we been asked what we need before doing the hard work of figuring out what we will have to have to accomplish our goals and mission? Nehemiah took the time to plan before setting out for Jerusalem and made it his first priority to survey the job before ever speaking to the people who were to help him.

One little correction about Nehemiah's priority upon arriving in Jerusalem. We should note that he did not go survey the wall until he had been in Jerusalem for three days. One of the greatest neglects of Christians, especially leaders, is the need for rest. After a ninety day journey from Susa to Jerusalem, Nehemiah realized that he needed rest before trying to survey the walls and make good decisions regarding the allocation of tasks and resources.

Sabbath rest is not just an Old Testament idea; we all need rest, and there is no substitute for it. God honors us when we set aside time to rest and reflect on Him and His goodness. This will both refresh us and remind us that He is our strength. We cannot just depend on our own abilities to push through to the completion of a task, or mission. Refueling our spirit in His Presence is always a necessity!

Nehemiah encouraged the people to remember God and fight for their families. When the walls were finished, his next priority was to reestablish proper worship by God's people in God's house. He elevated the Word of God and led the people to commit to obeying it and loving God and each other.

May we apply these principles to our lives in order to respond to the needs before us and our fellow believers to the glory of God!

Elijah

David Mason

"And Elijah the Tishbite, of the inhabitants of Gilead, said to Ahab, "As the Lord God of Israel lives, before whom I stand, there shall not be dew nor rain these years, except at my word." 1 Kings 17:1

In preparation for writing this devotional, I studied twelve of the prophets that are listed in the Bible. I looked at their spiritual strengths and weaknesses and how they were able to carry out the voice and direction of God. I found some of the prophets having a more significant impact than others, with character traits readily apparent. At the end of my research and to begin putting pen to paper, I chose God's prophet Elijah, as the one my character most resembled. Now let me say up front, I am not a prophet and do not pretend to be one. But in an apple to apples-to-apples comparison, I was able to look at the character of Elijah and determine, that yes, some of those same Christian strong points that defined Elijah, defined me as well.

I am a retired Federal Executive Employee working Benefits and Services programs for our nation's veterans and their families at the U.S. Department of Veterans Affairs in Washington DC. I will say that both jobs were the most responsible adventures I had ever engaged in, and my spiritual growth from when I first started in the Air Force was a lot stronger when I finished at Veterans Affairs in 2020. During my time in the Air Force, I was able to lead thousands of men and women in accomplishing whatever mission objectives our unit was tasked to accomplish. Whether it was training as part of operational nuclear deterrence activities or writing DoD Nuclear Policy and Guidelines for President Barack Obama, and congressional members.

Through it all, I served at the highest levels of our government. Over the course of 33 years, my most lasting memory of employment was being able to meet a lot of people and to make great friends along the way. My ability to work operations in the Air Force or on a staff position at VA did not define the person that I was. Being able to Lead People to accomplish a mission was my strongest core characteristic. Which brings us into the discussion about Elijah, and his effective leadership core competency.

Elijah was a mighty prophet during a turbulent time in Israel's history. The nation had turned away from the Lord to worship Baal, and King Ahab had formed an alliance with Sidon by marrying their princess, Jezebel. Elijah was sent to show Israel the evil of their ways and encourage them to return to the Lord.

Elijah had three main leadership traits:
- **Faith:** Elijah trusts that God will follow through on God's promises. And Elijah trusts his calling is from God.
- **Courage:** A prophet's call is never easy; Elijah's is no exception. He is to bring a message of condemnation to the most powerful person in the kingdom. Then, three years later, he returns. That takes courage, a courage born of faith.
- **Obedience:** Out of faith and courage, Elijah obeyed God's commands and followed through on his calling.

Faith and Obedience
Ever since growing up in the church back home in North Carolina, my faith in God has grown by leaps and bounds, and I know that anything I accomplish in this world we live in, is a direct blessing from God and is what He has ordained. Courage to live life as a prophet is another core character trait. The life of being a prophet is not easy, and it was Elijah's call to be a prophet. Lastly obedience… out of faith and cour-

age, Elijah obeyed God's commands. Being an obedient Christian and walking in the footsteps of Christ, and living a righteous life, is my daily journey as well. I will be honest; sometimes, I fail to hit the mark in living in obedience. But I do repent daily in asking for God's forgiveness in the sins that I have committed. There is only one person who has lived a life to perfection, and that is Christ. But the obedience of Elijah serves as valuable lesson that all Christians should follow.

God called Elijah to perform some very difficult and arduous activities. First, God sent him to King Ahab to tell the king there would be no rain or dew in the land of Israel for the next several years. Why? Because the northern kingdom of Israel had forsaken the Lord's commandments and given themselves over to unrestrained wickedness, atrocities, and idolatries.

Ahab, son of Omari, did evil in the sight of the Lord more than all who were before him. And as if it had been a light thing for him to walk in the sins of Jeroboam, son of Nebat, he took as his wife Jezebel, daughter of King Ethbaal of the Sidonians, and went and served Baal, and worshiped him. He erected an altar for Baal in the house of Baal, which he built in Samaria. Ahab also made a sacred pole. Ahab did more to provoke the anger of the Lord, the God of Israel, than had all the kings of Israel who were before him. Hmmm... married a foreign woman and worshipped her gods. Sounds a bit like Solomon's sin, don't you think? The task that the Lord gave to Elijah was very forward, so Elijah must have been trepid before speaking to the King. After all, Ahab was the ruling king over Israel, which gave him authority to have Elijah imprisoned, or even put to death.

Before Elijah proclaimed God's Word to Ahab, God had not yet told Elijah what would come next. Still, Elijah was obedient. Regardless of any fear or reservation, he performed the task that God told him to perform, which was to speak God's Word to Ahab and Israel. Then, Elijah waited and listened for the Lord to give him follow up instructions. Elijah followed God step-by-step. He was faithful in performing the tasks that God called him to perform, and then waiting patiently and listening to God for the next instruction. In our lives, we experience much and are called to perform many tasks, just as Elijah was asked to perform. And that exemplifies how we are to follow God's advice, step-by-step in obedience. Looking at the faithfulness and obedience of Elijah, both traits teach us and challenge us all at the same time. As followers of Christ, we are called to *"walk by faith, not by sight,"* 2 Corinthians 5:7, NKJV. But that can be difficult, I know. I have had my struggle with that throughout my lifetime. I know that this direction may cause us to be reluctant if we do not know the "complete picture" for what God is calling us to perform. Most of us will procrastinate because we want to know how the story ends from the beginning. But take faith in the matter that God calls us to follow Him, step-by-step.

Courage

There is no doubt that Elijah's faith and obedience prepared him to carry God's task of approaching King Ahab, but it can be argued that Elijah's courage was his strongest leadership trait of them all. Having courage is a trait that I pride myself in. Serving over two decades in the military in the Air Force and performing a mission and having the end of the world at my fingertips, was the most important task I have ever completed. But constant prayer and relying on God's faithful guidance to perform nuclear alerts without error, is what got me through the severity of the moments.

Sometimes, I still wonder, even to this day, if I would have had the same kind of courage that Elijah displayed in approaching King Ahab who had the ability to disregard my feedback from the Lord, and to kill me at his pleasure. But Elijah displayed a great amount of courage and showed that he was well up to the task given to him by God. As you know, Elijah obediently confronted Ahab, contested the prophets of Baal on Mount Carmel, and was threatened by Jezebel (which filled him with fear). But through it all, Elijah was ministered to by the Lord under the broom bush, and eventually continued to stand firm for the Lord until Ahab was finally killed in battle.

Having a high degree of courage is what paved the way for Elijah to perform as instructed by God. Which is like the task that our Lord has for all Christians. We are a *kind* of Elijah and have been consigned by our Lord to defend righteousness and confront evil. As servants of God, it is our responsibility and our assignment to courageously take a stand.

Taking a stand for the Lord is not always easy, or safe. When a contemporary of Elijah, the prophet Micaiah, son of Imlach, was called upon to confer with Ahab, he was urged to prophesy in agreement with the four hundred prophets of the King. But Micaiah courageously said, *"As surely as the Lord lives, I can tell him only what the Lord tells me"* 1 Kings 22:14.

Every day presents us with challenges—things we can take a stand for or against, issues that might not be too popular with some in the community, topics that might even stir up our congregants. As I have grown in my spirituality, I have found myself asking my inner self: "Will you take a stand, even if your words and actions displease people? Will you have the courage of Elijah to speak truth even if you become a target for people's hostility?"

My Journey as a Christian Leader

It is true that not all of us are leaders. But I would think, and past performances have proven, that I have been able to lead people. But now taking that same energy and drive in becoming an effective Christian leader, one who is in depth with scriptural knowledge is the task that I have before me. Sure, there are obvious leaders: pastors, CE leaders, and worship leaders in the Church and your bosses and political leaders elsewhere. But leadership is about guiding another person (or persons) along a certain path. Parents and guardians are leaders in their families. You might even be an informal leader among your friends. In whatever capacity you might be a leader (or may become someday), you can know and acknowledge that God has called you to this role. You can have faith that God will equip you with what you need. You take courage in God to do what needs to be done. And you can be obedient to this calling.

In my journeys of strengthening my Christian leadership, I am currently a Master of Divinity Degree student at Regent University. Once complete in summer of 2024, I will take the knowledge gained into becoming an effective church pastor. I have never believed that a person must pursue a master's degree before becoming a pastor, but for me, the schooling continually grows my knowledge of Scripture and educates me on overall pastoral responsibilities. I am confident that schooling will provide the necessary validation of education for my pastoral journey.

Once I become a church pastor, I will then go back to school and earn my PhD in Ministry. Once again, I am not saying that a person must obtain a degree to become an effective pastor, but for me, that educational journey will make me that much more effective in preaching God's Word.

Along the way, in all my efforts, I will always recall the story of the Prophet Elijah. The tremendous leadership and core characteristics that Elijah possessed, I, too, want to be viewed as being strong in those areas. Having the courage to speak out for what is right and maintain righteousness, and to have the faith and obedience that I will always adhere to God's Word.

Being a Christian is not an easy journey, I will tell everyone that. But I do know that all the struggles that we face, and that we will face, are meant to draw us closer to God. And that gives me great comfort at the end of the day.

David

Glen Allen Fox

"Then Samuel took the horn of oil and anointed him in the midst of his brothers; and the Spirit of the Lord came upon David from that day forward. So Samuel arose and went to Ramah." 1 Samuel 16:13

As King David began his walk with the severed head of the feared giant named Goliath in his hand, I could only imagine how exhilarated he must have felt… joyful in his spirit knowing that God had come through for him once again! Just as He did many times before out in the field, defeating the lion and the bear and protecting his sheep. But now, knowing the Lord has promoted him to another level of confidence in his walk with God as his victories translated to defeating giants, wicked ones at that. This very walk with the living God, which David delighted in so much, was developed through beautiful times of worship and praise to the God of Israel, the one true Lord and Creator, whom he loved. Perhaps it even crossed his mind for a moment that he would write a beautiful song unto the Lord about his victory. What an amazing man of God! What a paradox of personality. Here is a man who started out just a shepherd boy taking responsibility seriously about his job for the Lord, who was a writer of scripture songs unto the Lord. The "Psalms of David," we call them, although we know some were written by others.

Yet, in David's core being that fateful day, he realized he was a warrior on a battlefield. His objective was to lead men in the name of the God of Israel, Jehovah, the true Lord of lords! Yes, the one and only true God, who created Heaven and Earth changed his destiny as he was soon to become an anointed warrior king! There's so much in David's fascinating life. We find in the Holy Scriptures the victories, along with the defeats, and the trials and tribulations that David would endure. We learn from it all, the good and bad. When we look at any of the great Bible characters, there are lessons to be learned from their stories… beginning, middle, and end. In Scripture, we learn from the full spectrum of David's experience, the tragedies, and triumphs. The songs of worship David wrote provide many great examples of faith and heroism, along with how he dealt with his lowest points of defeat, lamenting before God and us with complete transparency. He fell into the sins of adultery and murder. Yet, even still, he is called "a man after God's own heart!" Something I have always loved about King David… he is real, and he is raw; he is relatable and recognizable; he is rebellious, yet he is redeemable; and in the end, he is restored, and he is counted righteous.

In reflecting on my own life, even in the beginning of my walk with God (41 years ago at the age of 19), my connection to David as prophet, poet, shepherd, king, and warrior resounds all the more. What I share here is not to boast about myself, because my only boast is in God, my own Creator who made me! When I repented for the first time and embraced Jesus Christ as my Lord and Savior, He then put His own Holy Spirit inside of me! Hallelujah! Again, I say, "Hallelujah! Anybody who knows me knows that I am never ashamed to praise God with all my heart and voice! And, when able, even at the age of 59, I love to dance before the Lord. The Scripture says *David danced before the Lord with all his might and with shouts of joy*, 2 Samuel 6:14. Maybe as a new Christian at age 19, I could have given David a run for his money, but now as my body ages, I certainly can't move with the fluidity I did before. Yet, I could tell you my heart continues this amazing dance of joy of my salvation, and the love, that even grows to this day. How could it not, when I consider that my dear God hung on the old, rugged Cross and bled out to cover my sins in order to redeem me back to the Father. I also can relate to King David when we see him repenting in Psalms 51:9-10, *"…blot out all my iniquity, create in me a pure heart oh*

God, and renew a steadfast spirit within me" Let us sing with David, "create in me a clean heart, oh God, and a right spirit within me."

The prophet Nathan called David out on his adultery and murder. Thankfully, I haven't murdered anyone, but in my desire to be transparent like David, I truly have had my battles here and there with sexual temptation. This was primarily when I was a young Christian. I "sowed my wild oats," made my mistakes and when I knew I was dishonoring the Cross and the Gospel, I repented and asked God for forgiveness. Quite often, I found myself doing everything I possibly could do to stay close to the heart of God. There were times when I never left the house of God and the courts of the Lord. I think of the verse Psalms 23:6, *"... surely your goodness and love will follow me all the days of my life, and I will dwell in the house of the Lord forever!"* That is my daily hope and prayer. I do love to be in the house of God many times each week. When the doors are open, I desire to be there. Honestly, and I say this without judgement, I don't understand why many Christians don't feel the same way. I want to go to church as often as possible because I want to meet with my God and feel His presence, especially when there's any kind of worship. As I said, I love to worship. Furthermore, I love to stand in the courts of praise with my Brothers and Sisters in Christ, the people of God. We will not forsake the holy assembly, especially as we see the days becoming more evil.

Although not intending to ever misuse the grace and mercy of God, I truly have needed God's mercy and grace after making missteps, great and small… simply, sin! Truly, if it wasn't for the goodness of God, those mistakes could have crushed me if it were not for the fact that the Lord's favor and protection have been over my life. I see clearly God was also protecting David and favoring him when he could've easily been destroyed, or killed. David sought the heart of God, and he truly found the heart of God and that goodness and mercy in kneeling at His feet. David didn't get judged to death after prophet Nathan called out his sin. And he easily could have been executed because his violations were severe. One of my favorite verses in the Bible is *"He who is forgiven much will love much"* Luke 7.47. Truly as David would write, I find myself saying, *"I love you, Lord, my Lord… the Lord is my Shepherd, and I shall not want!"* Psalm 23:1. My heart wants God! I still thank Our

Father in Heaven that my heart longs for Him, even now after a few decades, learning from my mistakes, dedicating my life, career, wife, family, home ministry, and the entirety of my future to His honor and Glory. May I love God even more for His daily provisions, which include my ever present need to be cleansed by the blood of Jesus, so that I would "walk in the light as He is in the light." In 1 John 1:7 we're all challenged to *"have fellowship one with another and the blood of Jesus will cleanse us from all our sins."* That includes you and that includes me.

Thank You, Jesus, for You are faithful and true, and You Yourself will return like the greatest warrior of all with that name written on Your thigh as You ride atop a great white horse! As You are getting ready to depart Your great throne in Heaven to return to this Earth, may all men (and women!) of God be truly ready to meet You, to join You, to serve You, to follow You, and to worship You. David knew the Lord is perfect and without sin. Now, I know that and I long for the day that the Lord will return. As it says in the Scripture: be expecting and be ready for the return of our Lord Jesus. Even Christ Himself said, *"So you must also be ready for you know not when the Son of Man will return"* Matthew 24:44. So because He said it, I believe it and it's good enough for me! May He find me faithful when He returns! If I depart first to meet Him in Glory, should He tarry, may I hear the words upon arrival, "Well done! Enter in!"

Actually, I didn't always know that there was a time for all seasons. Perhaps David was a teenager as well when he got the true revelation of who God really was, and just like me at the age of 18 prior to my 19th birthday, God opened my eyes to His greatness, and His mercy, and His love for me personally. No, I didn't write songs, but I certainly love to sing and praise in every song that I learned in church and to this day. I still remember most of them, or perhaps honestly, a good number of them. And I have also expressed my worship through poetry and have lifted high His name and His banner in some of the writings He has given me to share. There's nothing greater than praising God and worshiping God. There's nothing that prepares us more for Heaven.

David gives us a glimpse of what Heaven is really like and I can truly taste it. The Bible says, *"Taste and see that the Lord is good"* Psalms 34.8. When I worship God and delight in Him, even if I don't feel like doing it some days, just like David said in Psalms 103:1, we must encourage ourselves in the Lord and cry out with him: *"Bless the Lord oh my soul, and all that is within me bless his holy name bless the Lord oh my soul!"* Yes, David knew how to encourage himself in the Lord... that's what we all must do, too! I am doing that, especially now, as I am facing one of my biggest trials of my life. I could only describe it in a parallel sense with King David, when he made the tragic mistake of leaving his wife and children back at the camp in Ziklag, leaving it scarcely guarded as most of his fighting men went with to the battlefield only to come back to the unimaginable horror of all their wives and children taken captive.

Sadly, I let my guard down in my marriage and became too comfortable, just like David did. I took my wife and kids for granted at times, mostly my wife. So now, I, too, am in a similar current battle of my life for my family. Men of God, don't ever let your guard down; contend daily for the souls of your families. It is a war with the forces of darkness. Don't be complacent. Don't be lukewarm about God and all the things that matter to Him. Like David, with the Lord's help, strength, and His Holy Spirit leading and guiding me, I am going out daily on a "raiding party" to claim souls for the Kingdom and take territory for God. As I do, I intercede in the Spirit, that I find my family alive in Christ and that all is well with their souls like David did in 1 Samuel 30.

My testimony is not finished. The story continues. I'm on the journey. I'm on that road right now. I don't know the final chapter of my story in this regard, but I do have faith to believe because I know what God has done in giving me the past victories. I cannot say they're exactly the same, to the letter, as King David's because mine are spiritual battles, not physical ones. The Bible says we *"fight not against flesh and blood, but against principalities and powers and rulers, in high places"* Ephesians 6. But I know just the same God fights for me. The battle is the Lord's! There is a giant in front of me. (Truth be told, there is one in front of you... every believer, for that matter.) I cannot defeat him alone or think to even try, but I do know the God of Israel; the God of Abraham, Isaac, and Jacob does the fighting. I just have to do, like always, the believing and trusting, which counts the most… as right-eousness, for His Name's sake! When I turn to and trust in the Cross, and lift that prayer of faith, that stone will come out of its pouch! As I hurl it toward the enemy, it will hit its target square between the eyes, and the victory will be mine! Yet not mine only—truly God's victory is the only victory I could share. He gets all the glory and the honor and the praise! Hallelujah! Do you hear me? No matter what the end result is, it always must be proclaimed: "Hallelujah!" It constantly must be "Praise the Lord!" Saints, let us continually worship God, in the beauty of His Holiness!

In conclusion, let's remember that King David was a shepherd boy who became a warrior king, a poet and musician, and a man after God's own heart. His life was full of both victories and defeats, but through it all, he remained faithful to God. One of the things that I love the most about King David is his passion for God. He loved to worship God and sing His praises. He also wrote many beautiful psalms that are still cherished by Christians today. David's love for God was evident in everything he did. Another thing that I admire about King David is his courage. He was not afraid to stand up to Goliath, even though the giant was much bigger and stronger than he was. David knew that God was with him, and he trusted that God would give him the victory. Recall, in 1 Samuel 17:45-47, we read the story of David's victory over Goliath. This passage reminds us that God is with us, even when we face chal-lenges that seem impossible.

David also made mistakes. I could certainly relate to that, maybe not to that extent because he committed adultery with Bathsheba and had her husband killed. However, he was quick to repent and ask for God's forgiveness. When I fall, I try to do the same thing as much as possible. May I encourage all who are reading this, to turn back to God immedi-ately after you have fallen. All have fallen and come short of God's Glory… those who are wise will rise up and make the return trip to the Father's house and lay themselves at His altar… "I believe, help my unbelief. Help me to live for You because I cannot make it on my own!" God forgave David, and He used David's mistakes to teach him and to make him a better man. In Psalm 51, we read David's prayer of repentance after he committed adultery. This psalm reminds us that God is always willing to forgive us when we repent. I believe that we can all learn from the life of King David. I know I did and still do! We can learn to love God with all our hearts. This is a lifetime challenge, to be courageous, and to repent of our sins. We can also learn that God is faithful to forgive us when we fall short.

If you are facing a difficult challenge in your life, I encourage you to remember the story of King David. Remember his love for God, his courage, and his willingness to repent. Remember that God is faithful to forgive us and to help us overcome our challenges. With God's help, we can all live victorious lives, just like King David. I know that's what I will strive to continue to do until the Day of the Lord.

Peter

Eric Barbee

"And I tell you, you are Peter, and on this rock I will build my church, and the gates of hell shall not prevail against it." Matthew 16:18

I was not raised in a Christian home and had an abusive father. My sister and I witnessed my mother go through things that no child should ever see. We moved from North Carolina to Virginia when I was in the 5th grade. Our parents put us in a Christian school and that was the first time I accepted Christ as my Savior. We moved back to North Carolina the following year. We were not involved in church; however, I knew I had a relationship with God.

In my 9th grade year, we headed back to Virginia for good. We went to a public high school and I excelled in my freshman and sophomore years. I was involved in soccer, went to the Governors Magnet school, and was very involved in theater, and made good grades. I was popular in high school, had many friends, dated pretty girls, and was a really good soccer player. My parents divorced when I was sixteen, and I became very rebellious. I started hanging out with a group of guys that regularly did drugs, and drank. I was arrested but never charged four different times from being with this crowd.

Even though I was partying everyday—smoking pot and drinking with friends—I knew that wasn't what God wanted and I was always praying for a way out. I was even considering moving back to North Carolina with my dad just to get away from it all.

At nineteen years old, on April 22, 1989, I left from my mom's house late at night to ride with a friend to his home an hour and a half away. I was the passenger in the front seat of his new 88 Camaro without a seatbelt on. I asked him to let me drive, but his father said no one else could drive his new car. I fell asleep on the way there and he feel asleep behind the wheel about an hour down the road. We crashed into a metal telephone poll and they say I was thrown into the dashboard. To this day, I still do not remember a thing. I was taken to the hospital and then flown by helicopter to a larger hospital in Richmond, Virginia. The doctor told my mother that night they weren't sure I was going to make it. I laid in a coma for nine days and was in the hospital 2 ½ months. I went through physical therapy to learn to walk again and occupational therapy to work on my motor skills.

After I woke up from the coma, my mom would get me in my wheelchair and go down to the chapel every Sunday that I was in the hospital. When I was able to wheel myself, I remember one day in my hospital room the Lord speaking to me—clear as can be. He said, "I've given you a second chance, what are you going to do with it?" I promised the Lord that day I would live for Him.

"And if it seems evil to you to serve the Lord, choose for yourselves this day whom you will serve, whether the gods which your fathers served that were on the other side of the River, or the gods of the Amorites, in whose land you dwell. But as for me and my house, we will serve the Lord" Joshua 24:15

Let me go back a little: While I was in the coma, I had a Nazarene pastor from my hometown that didn't know me, but had a church member that was friends with my mother, come visit me. That church had been praying for me and the pastor would come and hold my hand and sing and pray over me while I was in a coma. I was released after 2 ½ months and went home. I started attending that Nazarene church where the pastor that visited me preached. I was baptized within a year and became the youth leader after four years of attending that church. I later became the lay pastor for the church and when my preacher was called to another state and we were without a pastor, I took over Wednesday night services and some Sunday evening services. I never had any desire to go back to my old lifestyle.

"And Jesus, walking by the Sea of Galilee, saw two brothers, Simon called Peter, and Andrew his brother, casting a net into the sea; for they were fishermen. Then He said to them, "Follow Me, and I will make you fishers of men." They immediately left their nets and followed Him "
Matthew 4:18-20

Jesus called Simon (Peter) and his brother, Andrew, out of their comfort zone and familiar surroundings to follow Him, to drop every-thing they were doing, to leave their profession and their families, so He could make them "fishers of men". I did not fully know it then, but God was calling me to do the same. He wanted me to leave my old lifestyle and habits to follow Him and spread His Gospel to all that would hear. He saved me and allowed me to live after all that I had done with my life as a teenager, and He wanted me to use my testimony to share with others who He is and how much He loves us.

I was part of the Nazarene church for eighteen years and even went to school to be ordained. I've taught Sunday School classes for the last thirty-four years and am still preaching God's Word. I've just become the associate pastor of a small church in my hometown that I've been attending outside my regular church for thirteen years. It seems I am doing exactly what God called Peter to do, and that is being a "fisher of men". I never thought in my wildest dreams that I would be preaching the Gospel of Jesus Christ and leading others to His saving grace. I am sure Peter did not think he would be one of the disciples to walk with Jesus, the Messiah, either. Peter was considered a very bold and brash man; his mouth was always getting him in trouble and he didn't hold his tongue for anyone. He was known as a "hothead" amongst his people. It is amazing to see how God calls us even in our sinful state to come and follow Him. We see Peter, even after walking with Jesus for a while, threatening to cut off the ear of the high priest's servant that was there to detain Jesus.

"Then Simon Peter, having a sword, drew it and struck the high priest's servant, and cut off his right ear. The servant's name was Malchus. So Jesus said to Peter, "Put your sword into the sheath. Shall I not drink the cup which My Father has given Me?" John 18:10-11

I have a scar on my forehead and right eye from the accident. Although it almost killed me, I wouldn't change a thing. Had I lost my life on April 22, 1989, and stood before the Lord and He asked me, "Why should I let you into My Kingdom?" I wouldn't have had an answer and that scares me for others who are in the same shoes I was. I was a believer, but so is Satan. I now have a personal relationship with my Lord and Savior that will never go away. I have shared my testimony many times in youth groups, churches, schools, and just personal conversations. I try to tell everyone that hears my story to wear your seatbelts, and live each day like it's your last because you never know when it could be and don't believe one of the enemy's biggest lies and that is, "You've got plenty of time to get your life right. Just keep living the way you are for now."

Peter walked with Jesus but still denied Him when questioned if he knew Him. Jesus told Peter that he would deny Him three times before the rooster crowed. Even after doing exactly what Jesus said he would do, He did not give up on Peter. Peter wept bitterly at his actions and was surely convicted. Be sure that you don't allow your heart to become hardened where you don't sense the need to repent and turn to God. Peter did not really believe that Jesus was going to die on the Cross that day, and even tried to prevent it. Yet, it all happened exactly as Jesus had prophesied to them all.

Regardless of Peter's weaknesses, his faith is considered the foundation of the Church!

"When Jesus came into the region of Caesarea Philippi, He asked His disciples, saying, "Who do men say that I, the Son of Man, am?" So they said, "Some say John the Baptist, some Elijah, and others Jeremiah or one of the prophets." He said to them, "But who do you say that I am?" Simon Peter answered and said, "You are the Christ, the Son of the living God." Jesus answered and said to him, "Blessed are you,

PETER

Simon Bar-Jonah, for flesh and blood has not revealed this to you, but My Father who is in heaven. And I also say to you that you are Peter, and on this rock I will build My church, and the gates of Hades shall not prevail against it. And I will give you the keys of the kingdom of heaven, and whatever you bind on earth will be bound in heaven, and whatever you loose on earth will be loosed in heaven" Matthew 16:13-19

God does promise us that He will never leave or forsake us and that's a truth you can hold onto but when your last day comes, of which none of us know, will you be ready? Who will you say He is? Will you receive Him into your heart today? I did, and my life has never been the same!

"For I know the thoughts that I think toward you, says the LORD, thoughts of peace and not of evil, to give you a future and a hope" Jeremiah 29:11-13.

Joseph

Anthony K. Gantt

"Now Israel loved Joseph more than all his children, because he was the son of his old age: and he made him a coat of many colors." Genesis 37:3

J oseph faced significant hardships, including being sold into slavery by his own family and unjustly imprisoned in Egypt. Despite these challenges, he maintained his faith and integrity, eventually rising above his situation/situations and into a position of power where he had the ability to save nations from famine. Like Joseph, I am going to show you how I encounter trials in my life and in comparing our stories, hopefully, it will remind us of the importance of perseverance, faith, and making the best of difficult situations.

"Beloved, do not think it strange concerning the fiery trial, which is to try you, as though some strange thing happened to you; but rejoice to the extent that you partake in Christ's suffering, that when his glory is revealed, you may also be glad with exceeding joy" 1 Peter 4:12–13, NKJV.

I was born of two teenage parents, my mother was fifteen years old, and my father was sixteen. When you have two teenagers at such an early age having children and being promiscuous, one can only imagine the dysfunction that may be in their families. My father was raised in a single mother home with five other siblings and my mother was raised with both parents, but her father was physically and sexually abusive in every way. When you put these ingredients together, it tends to be a recipe for disaster. Although my parents were teenagers, they had to grow up fast. They were in no way in a position to care for an infant child when both were still dependent on their parents. My mother was one of twelve children that grew up in a five-bedroom rowhouse on 16th and Catherine Street in South Philadelphia. She grew up seeing the man that was supposed to protect her physically abusing her mother and sexually abusing her and her siblings. Unlike Joseph, my family did not throw me down a well or sell me to Egypt; however, there was a sense of betrayal that those who were supposed to protect you and keep you safe were the ones that wanted to do harm to you. Because of these issues that my mother had to go through with her environment at home, she became wrapped up in drugs; it first started with marijuana, and it ended up with crack. She became homeless and strung out and I had to move in to my father's house with his wife and their children. That is when I became the "stepchild."

Joseph and his siblings shared the same father; however, out of his twelve siblings, he only shared his mother with one, his youngest brother, Benjamin. The Bible talks about how Joseph was hated by his brothers so much that they could only speak ill of him, Genesis 37:4. My siblings did not "hate" me; however, they would make fun of me and tease me because I did not fit in, and I was not like them. They grew up having both parents in the home and I was this emotionally broken, street smart, dirty boy that was injected into their lives and way of living. They grew up with Muslim values, did not use profanity, never ate pork products, and had good grades in school. However, I grew up with different values; meaning, I used profanity, ate pork products, was not a good student in school, and had my fair share of watching inappropriate movies with little to no oversight. Because of this vastly different lifestyle, I quickly became the *black sheep* and *outsider* of all the chil-dren. It was so bad, whenever I would use a bowl, cup, fork, or spoon from the kitchen, my siblings would say to each other, "Don't eat out of that bowl or use that spoon/fork, because Tony ate off them," or my stepmother discreetly giving me less food than my siblings. I remember when we all gathered in the kitchen for ice cream on a cone, everyone else had two scoops and I was only given one scoop. I did not understand why they were treating me like this, and I started to blame and resent my mother for putting me in this situation. Just like Joseph, this situation became my pit experience. I did not understand how and why I ended up here, I just knew that this was the lowest point of my life, and I did not know how I was going to get out.

Joseph's brothers stripped him of his coat of many colors. His coat of many colors was the mark of honor and rank, worn only by the chief and heir. Joseph inherited that birthright as the beloved favorite child of Jacob. The proverbial "coat of many colors," as the oldest child in my father's house, was also taken away from me. I moved into his house and was treated as a stepchild; I felt like my birthright as his first born was removed and I felt like I was not even a part of his family. I can only imagine how Joseph felt when he was thrown into the pit and betrayed by those who were supposed to love and protect him, to later be sold into Egypt.

"THE LORD WAS WITH JOSEPH"

"And the Lord was with Joseph, and he was a prosperous man; and he was in the House of his master the Egyptian. And his master saw that the Lord was with him, and that the Lord made all that he did to prosper in his hand" Genesis 39: 2-3, KJV.

Joseph's early life was marked by betrayal by his brothers, who were jealous of him. If you have ever experienced betrayal, or been hurt by those close to you, Joseph's story shows the power of forgiveness and reconciliation. Despite what his brothers did, Joseph chose to forgive them to provide for their needs when they were in distress. I hated my mother for many years because I blamed her and her addiction for putting me in this situation with my father and his family. I felt like she put the drugs and her own needs before the needs of her children. I was only ten years old, and I did not understand the consequences and effects of addiction. Especially the addiction to crack in the height of the crack endemic.

I remember vividly walking home from school one day and seeing my mother on the corner of 16th Street. I had not seen my mother in over six months due to her being homeless and strung out. I saw her hair was messy, she was frail, and had what looked like a light tannish grey trench coat wrapped around her as if it were a robe that went past her knees in the middle of spring. I screamed, "Mom! Mom!" She turned around and saw me, and I ran to her and gave her a hug. She smelled of old stale cigarettes, dirty clothes, and musty. Her face looked tired, worn, and like she had not slept in weeks. I told her how I missed her, and she said she missed me, too. Right as she was saying she missed me, her drug dealer walked up behind her with the product she had been looking for and waiting for. She looked at the dealer then she looked at me and told me to "take a walk." I had not seen her in six months and after five minutes of reuniting, she told me to "take a walk." This was a betrayal that would take me years to get over and delivered from. This was the beginning of my *Egypt experience*.

Egypt in the Bible, for New Testament believers, represents the world or a life of slavery and sin/sinful nature. During the ages of 10-17, I became an angry young man. I became promiscuous and was also a victim of sexual assault and molestation by family members. Although I was going through such turmoil, I knew the Lord was with me. There were many occasions during my life to where the consequences could have been a lot worse than they were. I believe it is because the Lord was with me.

Joseph was sold into slavery, purchased by an officer of Pharaoh named Potiphar, and molested by Potiphar's wife. Although Joseph went through these painful experiences, the Bible says that Joseph was a prosperous man and everything his hands touched prospered, Genesis 39:2-3. God was with him! Although we go through trauma in our own lives, we must understand that the Lord is our rock, our fortress, our deliverer, our guide, and our strength in whom we must trust. Therefore, our eyes should look unto the hills from where our help comes from, knowing that our help comes from the Lord, Psalm 121:1. As believers, that is how we can be prosperous in the midst of our storms; this is how we can be prosperous in the midst of our trials and our tribulations just as Joseph was. Although Joseph went through all that he endured, the Bible does not say anything about how Joseph held on to unforgiveness for the people that wronged him in his life. His brothers throwing him into a pit and Potiphar's wife getting him thrown into prison was all in preparation for his reign in the palace (place of leadership and responsibility).

Just like Joseph, I hold no unforgiveness in my heart for the people who wronged me in my life. I have fully forgiven those family members who have hurt me physically, emotionally, and sexually. I can absolutely say, with full assurance, that I forgive them. I had people in my life who would always pray for me, take me to church, and constantly plant the Word of God in my heart throughout all my hardships.

"Therefore, if anyone is in Christ, he is a new creation; all things have passed away; Behold, all things have become new." 2 Corinthians 5:17, NKJV.

Throughout Joseph's trials, he remained faithful and maintained his integrity, which played a crucial role in his eventual success in the fulfillment of God's plan for his life. Our faith in our belief embodies integrity, which mandates us to stay true to God's principles.

After graduating from high school, at 17 years old, I enlisted in the United States Army on August 20th of 1993. The military is where I received a firm foundation on leadership, respect, integrity, and honor. It played a significant role in my walk with Christ. On December 29, 2001, I received Salvation and was born again at Victory Through Faith Christian Fellowship in Kitzingen, Germany. This, through all the other trials and tribulations in my life, was all to prepare me for this moment in my walk with Christ and now, I'm in my *palace experience* as an Executive at my job, been married to the same woman for 24 years, my children are flourishing, and I have been blessed living in four different states (Alaska, Missouri, Oklahoma, and Texas). To God be the Glory!

Like Joseph, we are all subject to life's unpredictable nature, where moments of joy can swiftly turn to trials. Yet, it is through these trials that our character is tested, and our resilience is built. Joseph's ability to forgive his brothers, despite their grave betrayal, teaches us this transformative power of forgiveness not just for those who wrong us, but for our own peace and liberation from the past. Moreover, Joseph's journey from a dreamer and becoming a ruler in Egypt highlights the importance of recognizing and nurturing our gifts. Even when their purpose is not immediately clear, our talents and dreams have the potential to lead us to our destiny, serving not only our own personal growth, but also the betterment of those around us. The divine Providence evident in Joseph's life reminds us that there is often a bigger picture to our struggles, a plan that we may not understand until we look back upon our journey. This perspective encourages us to maintain faith and hope, even when the path forward is obscured by the immediate pain of the present.

Enjoying parallels between Joseph's story and my own, I am reminded that the essence of life is not found in the absence of challenges but in how we respond to them. It is in our capacity to endure, to forgive, to grow, and to find meaning in the midst of trials that we truly reflect the spirit of Joseph's legacy. As I move forward in my own journey, I carry with me the lessons of resilience, faith, forgiveness, and the pursuit of purpose, inspired by Joseph's example to navigate life's valleys and mountaintops with grace and courage.

"Therefore, if anyone is in Christ, he is a new creation; all things have passed away; Behold, all things have become new," 2 Corinthians 5:17, NKJV.

Samuel

Steven Cartwright

"Now the Lord said to Samuel, "How long will you mourn for Saul, seeing I have rejected him from reigning over Israel? Fill your horn with oil, and go; I am sending you to Jesse the Bethlehemite. For I have provided Myself a king among his sons." 1 Samuel 16:1

The Prophet Samuel is a pivotal figure in the scriptures. In spending time studying his life, I like to call him *the Great Facilitator*, because of the significant movements and shifts in the narrative of Scripture, the history of Israel, and the legacy of our faith that he is assigned to oversee. It is during Samuel's time that the nation of Israel goes from being a theocracy to essentially becoming a monarchy. This moves them from the time of the judges and priests to the time of the kings and prophets. He then becomes the last judge and the first prophet of Israel. He anoints Israel's first king, which we could call the "King of Men," and Israel's second King, known as *God's King*. All of these shifts are prophetic in that they offer us type figures of our Messiah as Prophet, Priest, and King.

His life itself begins as the result of pivotal prayers that are offered up by his mother, Hannah, in 1Samuel 1:1-28. Her prayers were courageous enough to petition God for a child even though her body was physically incapable of producing children. The question is why believe, and why even ask? She asked because she believed in God who hears our prayers. In 1 Samuel 1:27 she says: *"For this child I prayed; and the LORD has given me my petition which I asked of him."* It is a wonderful thing that God hears our prayers. The birth of Samuel is an example of this. If we are courageous enough to ask, He is faithful enough to hear and give us what we ask of Him according to His will, 1 John 5:14,15. Samuel lived because God hears our prayers.

I remember when my wife and I started our ministry *The Refuge of Denver*. One of the elements of our worship experience that the Lord led us to include was *prayer*. Technically, this was not anything novel, because every church prays on Sundays; but for us, it was unique because the time of prayer would not be something done an hour before service. It would actually be done within the worship experience itself. So, we didn't have thirty minutes of prayer before our service started. We had thirty minutes of prayer to start the worship experience. Prayer and intercession was set to be the beginning and foundation of our service. This was pivotal for me because I never viewed myself as uniquely gifted for intercession, but God did. This really started to shape me personally and in my ministry in a different way than I was used to because God began to illuminate revelation to me about prayer and intercession.

This was especially experienced during the 2020 pandemic when we could not meet physically and so I would do times of prayer virtually through social media. Prayer became even more vital for all of us and during that time; I began to go deeper into the space of prayer and intercession. Sitting in atmospheres where prayer was being exhibited and taught really strengthened me in this area and is one of the reasons why the Prophet Samuel is so appealing to me today. One key element that I began to realize is that prayer is as much about hearing and listening as it is about speaking and petitioning. Impactful prayer is always defined by what you hear after you have prayed, as much as what you have said in the discourse of praying. Being *Heard by God* is the first part, and *Hearing God* is the second the part.

The movement of Samuel's life and ministry has, at its core, the Power of Hearing and Being Heard. If the prayers of his mother were his life's first pivotal moment, then 1 Samuel chapter 3 is his second. But this time, it is not about God Hearing Samuel, but Samuel Hearing God. Samuel goes through a series of encounters that involve him hearing the call of God. The Lord says, *"Samuel, Samuel"* three times and each time, he confuses God's voice with the voice of his spiritual father, Eli, 1 Samuel 3:4-7. On the third time around, Eli realizes that it is God calling and gives Samuel his first set of important instructions: *"When you hear Him, answer this way: Speak Lord for your servant is listening,"* 1 Samuel 3:8-9. If we are going to hear God's call, then our whole spirit, soul, and body must be open to listen for His Word.

It is most important that after hearing God's call, we listen to His voice for wisdom. Hearing is the beginning of listening, and so he goes from hearing to listening. It is at this point that God gives Samuel a message that is a truth and a challenge at the same time. It is God's Truth because His Word is truth, absolutely and never partially, John 17:17. It is God's challenge because it is a message of judgment directed towards Samuel's spiritual father, Eli, who is Israel's current high priest. When it is time to relay God's message, Eli, realizing the struggle Samuel has to have this courageous conversation with him, gives Samuel the second and most important instruction of his assignment. He essentially told him to *"Say everything God has told you and leave nothing out,"* 1 Samuel 3:15-18. This second set of instructions from Eli is the third point of prayer and intercession I want to share: "Do everything He says and leave nothing out." Prayer has this operational rhythm about it: Pray, Hear, Do. It is the cycle of prayer we should pursue to follow always.

So, Samuel spoke all of God's Word completely to Eli, leaving nothing out, and it was at this point that Samuel pivoted and became the first official Prophet of Israel. Because he followed these instructions all his life, it was said that none of his words fell to the ground, 1 Samuel 3:19-21. He has to Hear the Call, Listen to the Word, and then Relay the Message thoroughly and completely. This is the operational rhythm of the Office of the Prophet, and a functional necessity of all believers. This operation puts Samuel not only in the Office of the Prophet, but also in the place of the intercessor. To me, this is what makes him a facilitator; standing in the gap between where we are and where God wants us to be, and being instrumental in God's process to get us there. Herein is where we find the true ministry of prayer. It is when it goes beyond the petitions given for our own benefit and moves into the faithful prayers offered on behalf of others. It has, as its core strength, the elements of speaking, hearing, and doing; hearing, listening, and relaying. What I have found is that these elements have to be built into your personal life and walk with God in order for them to take effect in your public ministry. Samuel knew God's voice for himself, personally. This is why God could trust him to facilitate His Kingdom agenda publicly. He knew God and was sensitive to hearing His voice.

When we look at 1 Samuel chapter 16, it is natural that we focus our attention on what God is saying and doing for the man He has chosen, David. But I want to take a minute and focus on the man God chooses to facilitate this exchange through, Samuel. He is the one who has become the mouthpiece of God. The one who has developed such a sensitive ear to hear the voice of God that he is able to communicate with God in the heat of the moment and so fulfill his present assignment of anointing the next king of Israel. There are four distinct moments where the voice of God guides Samuel through this process. Read 1 Samuel 16:1, 2, 7, and 12. Three times begin with this saying: *"And The Lord Said."* While one time begins with this saying, *"But the Lord said,"* and with each time that Samuel is able to hear what God says, he is able to fulfill his current assignment. Anyone that knows me, knows about my relationship with God through prayer. What I know is this: If the beginning of prayer is speaking, then the end of prayer is hearing. It is at the moment that we hear God that we can pivot, shift, and move the direction of our lives and the lives of others into the direction that He so desires for us.

Lastly, it is an emphasis on His desire that will be my fourth and final point for us today. We have talked about these points so far: 1. Praying, 2. Hearing, 3. Doing as the full cycle of prayer. When we step into a true place of prayer and intercession, we will realize that the developmental work of prayer is for us to pray prayers and build lives that are centered in God's desire for us. That's the fourth point. The wrap around point: God's desire and not our desire for our lives. That's the secret of true prayer and intercession. It is never really about us, though it starts with us.

SAMUEL

The true intercessor, prophet, facilitator, and child of God is completely submitted to these types of statements: *"Not my will but Yours be done,"* Matthew 26:39, and *"Let Thy Kingdom come and Thy will be done on Earth as it is in Heaven,"* Matthew 6:10. This is why Hannah prayed for a child and ended up with a prophet. Here is why none of the prophet's words fell to the ground. He was not speaking his words; He was speaking God's words. His heart was that the heart of the Father be made known and manifested in the realm of the Earth.

Our heart must be the same. If you relate to God in prayer, then your heartbeat is always: "Lord, let Your will be done." This is the blessing and benefit of a God who hears His people, and a people who hear their God.

John, the Beloved

Darrel Thompson, II

"Going on from there, He saw two other brothers, James the son of Zebedee, and John his brother, in the boat with Zebedee their father, mending their nets. He called them," Matthew 4:21

The Apostle of Love wasn't always loving. Did you know that John was selfish? Did you know that John had a major ego problem? Historically, John hated being corrected, had a bad temper, an appetite for revenge, was critical of people, and was very impulsive. The scripture gives examples of those characteristics. In Luke 9:49-50, John told Jesus that he and his fellow disciples had forbidden a non-disciple from casting out demons in Jesus' name. Jesus responds by making it clear that anyone who is not against them should be considered a friend. This example shows that John's focus was selfish, or possibly even jealous. He was not focused on the freedom this man could have; he was more focused on the person who was bringing the freedom.

His character is shown once again in Mark 10:35-40. John and his brother James, along with their mother, approached Jesus and requested that they get seats of honor by asking if they could sit to the right and left of Jesus' throne in His Kingdom. Jesus responds with His own questions. He asked them if they could drink from the same cup of suffering that He was going to drink and if they could endure the same baptism into death that Jesus knew He was going to experience. Jesus was focused on how they were going to live the rest of their lives, not the seat of honor itself. Once again, John was walking in a selfish identity, and everything in his life seemed to be for personal gain.

Another scripture that points to John's pre-love identity is Luke 9:51-56. In this passage, Jesus sent His disciples ahead of Him to ask if they could enter Samaria on their way to worship in Jerusalem. The Samaritans refused to allow Jesus and His disciples to enter. In response to that, James' and John's first instincts were to ask Jesus to call fire down from Heaven to kill the Samaritans. Jesus' response clearly revealed what was the nature of John's heart, but Jesus also used that as an opportunity to reveal His purpose on the Earth.

"Jesus rebuked them sharply, saying "Don't you realize what spews from your hearts when you say that? The Son of Man did not come to destroy life, but to bring life to the earth" Luke 9:55, TPT.

John's response was full of revenge, impulsiveness, and a lack of love. Have you ever thought about what transpired to cause John to transition from John "the son of thunder" to John "the beloved?" The Greek translation of son of thunder is *Boanerges*. This word can be translated as "sons of commotion" and means easily angered. This word is derived from the Aramaic word for rage. What was it that John saw in Jesus that made his identity change from a son of rage to an Apostle of love? He saw Jesus' kindness, compassion, mercy, and love and slowly became "the one whom Jesus loved."

John's identity began to change as he was pulled into love by the proximity he had with Jesus. Jesus pulled John close, and John didn't resist. He encountered the love of Yahweh by being present with Jesus during many of Jesus' intimate moments. John was there when Jesus raised Jairus' daughter back to life. John was also one of the three disciples who witnessed Jesus' transfiguration. He sat at the right-hand side of Jesus at the Passover meal, where Jesus intimately revealed to John that Judas would betray him. At Jesus' crucifixion, John was the only disciple there. Jesus used that moment to declare to Mary that John was now her son and to John that Mary was now his mother.

He saw firsthand that Jesus' mercy was bestowed on people who once would have been considered underserving, like the woman at the well. In the moments where judgment and wrath should have been poured out, he saw Jesus' kindness instead. A perfect example of this is seen in the story of the prostitute who was brought to Jesus to be stoned but was instead released with grace. John was also present when the woman was healed with the issue of blood. He saw the mercy of Jesus to heal a woman who would have been considered unclean. In the garden of Gethsemane, at Jesus' arrest, John witnessed Jesus heal a man's ear after Peter had pulled out a sword and cut off his ear. This was done to defend and protect Jesus. Instead of Jesus taking revenge and defending Himself, His kindness was given to even those who were there to arrest Him. This moment must have spoken to John, showing that rage, temper, and revenge could no longer be a part of his identity. John's closeness to Jesus allowed him to see the character, nature, and love of Yahweh through Christ.

Why is identity important? How you see yourself in Christ will determine how you look at those around you. If you don't see yourself correctly through Christ, you won't be able to see others correctly, either. I have a similar story and feel as though I can relate very closely to John.

In the early years of my life, I was often referred to as a "son of thunder." For a time, I wore those words as a badge of honor. Identifying as a "son of thunder" made me feel that speaking the hard things, even if they were overly harsh and offensive, was the correct way to approach people. I felt that as a "son of thunder," I should fight for what I believed in, but that fighting often lacked compromise, understanding, and love. I was selfish, self-promoting, easily angered, and communicated with a sharp and harsh tone. I often preached from a place of judgment towards others and made sure the storyline fit the narrative of my selfish nature. I was always looking out for myself, making sure that I always looked right, even at the expense of others. Although I didn't realize it at the time, there was an element of me that was reminiscent of a Pharisee. I believed I was loving Yahweh with my life, but instead, I was promoting a gospel that focused on keeping the law and being afraid of the Judgement of the Lord; yet this gospel was void of the very love I believed I was giving.

During this time, I owned my own business and was considered very successful. I was a multi-millionaire. My wife and I had planted a successful church, and I was very content with my life. Nonetheless, my wilderness season came. The Lord dragged me into the wilderness and began to work on the old nature inside of me. I was stripped of everything. I had to sell my business for pennies on the dollar, and I lost my home. Honestly, it felt like we had lost everything. The only thing that remained was our church, but it soon became its own kind of mess. I often felt like walking away from it all and even attempted to leave the ministry on numerous occasions.

Through this stripping, He began to deal with me in the area of love. When everything was gone, I found that closeness to Jesus was the only thing that got me through my daily life. His presence was no longer an option; it was a necessity. He became my daily bread. I found the way to get close to Him was through devotional intimacy. His love sustained me in a way that nothing else ever had. No amount of following the law or avoiding judgment made me healed. It was only by the closeness to His love that I found myself becoming restored and whole again. I had always avoided teaching on love because I was afraid people would pervert it and use it as an excuse to live however they wanted to. But, in the middle of the wilderness, I found that Jesus wasn't there to condemn me but to change me into a man who was full of love—a man who loved Jesus and loved His people.

The wilderness is a place that many long to avoid, but it has developed into a place that has become home to me. It is a place where I met Yahweh. Just as Moses was told by Yahweh to bring the children of Israel into the wilderness where He was, that is where I was being called to go. It was in the wilderness that Yahweh stripped me of all I thought I was. He dealt with my anger, pride, selfishness, and lack of love. The wilderness is where I began to see things through HIS eyes, and I was met by love. I couldn't love others because I didn't love myself. No one could measure up to my expectations because I didn't measure up to my own expectations. The wilderness is where I was led to go and die, die to myself. It was where I found grace, mercy, compassion, and peace. It was where I found beloved identity. It was where I found myself, through His eyes. I found that He loves me on my worst day just as much as He does on my best day. Ironically, my name Darrel means "beloved." I was no longer a "son of thunder," but "one whom Jesus loves." The wilderness is not a place I ever want to leave. I found through beloved identity that my wilderness had become a flowering garden, a garden that never wilts or withers.

Once your identity changes, you are never the same. John was never the same, and that was evident throughout the rest of his life. He became a pillar for the early church and was present during many miracles that were performed alongside Peter. He devoted his life to the instruction and equipping of the Church. He was even persecuted and imprisoned with Peter, yet joy and love remained a catalyst of his life.

All his letters to the Church were written from a place of beloved identity and point the readers to Christ and the importance of fellowship with Him. In the Book of 1 John, he reveals who Jesus is and who we have become in Him. In this letter, he teaches that we are to be ministers of love in how we walk in this life while demonstrating truth and kindness to all. In 2 John, he points his readers to truth and encourages all to hold it fast and never let it go. The theme of 2 John is "loving truth," and he teaches how truth generates love and that love will always be faithful to the truth. John taught believers to walk in love because walking in love is to walk into the truth of Yahweh! In his letter 3 John, he addressed the problems that can arise within hospitality. John desired that his sons and daughters in the faith be welcoming spirits, pouring out love and support for the sake of others. John believed hospitality was a way of expressing Christian love and warned against those who denied hospitality and stirred up trouble within the body. John also wrote Revelation. In this book, John unveils a beautiful Christ, and an overcoming company of saints is seen rising into His fullness. In all of John's writings, it is evident that the motivation and inspiration is love.

John was present during many of Jesus' teachings, including Jesus' teachings on love. One of the most important passages in the Bible was written in John 13. Verses 34 and 35 state, *"So I give you now a new commandment: Love each other just as much as I have loved you. For when you demonstrate the same love I have for you by loving one another, everyone will know that you're my true followers" TPT.*

85

This scripture summarizes the change that was seen in John after he lived in closeness to Christ. John let love and nearness to Christ change him from the inside. He began to see himself as beloved, just as I did. He realized that love was the true witness to others, not a fiery man who could follow the letter of the law. Loving one another was the expression of a true follower. Have you ever found yourself in a wilderness season? Can you relate to John as a "son of thunder?" If so, you are right where Yahweh wants you to be. When you have encountered the love of Yahweh, everything changes. The Bible teaches us that Yahweh is love. When John wrote those words, he meant every activity of Yahweh is filtered through love. In other words, Yahweh cannot do anything unloving because love is His very nature. So, embrace the road to the wilderness with joy. Know that Yahweh is not taking you there to hurt you, but to make you whole. He is longing to bring you into your original created purpose. That purpose is to bear His image. You and I can only bear His image by knowing His love. Love changes you into who you are meant to be. Love must be the motivation of our lives.

1 Corinthians 13 teaches us all about that love. It teaches us that love is patient, it is kind, and it is gentle. Love never rejoices in the shame of others; instead, love covers. Love always celebrates honesty and is never easily irritated. Love is the place we always go to find shelter. Love never takes failure as defeat because it never gives up. Love never ever stops loving because it is eternal. This is what we are called to walk in towards others. We are to walk in the same kind of love that chased after us. That unwavering love is what John encountered and what I encountered. That kind of love changed how John and I saw ourselves. Through that love, we see ourselves as beloved sons of Yahweh.

One of my favorite verses of Scripture is Romans 8:19. This passage says, *"The entire universe is standing on tiptoe yearning to see the unveiling of God's glorious sons and daughters" TPT.* Could it really be that all the Universe is waiting on is Yahweh's sons and daughters to encounter His love, so that they can be unveiled on the Earth? Imagine the Gospel preached to the cosmos from sons and daughters who live in beloved identity, living life through the lens of love. I can see it! I believe the unveiling is imminent. Can you see it? If you can, embrace the journey to a life changed by love.

Isaac

Barry Gott

"Then God said: "No, Sarah your wife shall bear you a son, and you shall call his name Isaac; I will establish My covenant with him for an everlasting covenant, and with his descendants after him." Genesis 17:19

The Sacrifice

Paul is simply extending the command of Jesus as it pertains to becoming a follower of The Christ.

"I beseech you therefore, brethren, by the mercies of God, that you present your bodies a living sacrifice, holy, acceptable to God, which is your reasonable service. And do not be conformed to this world, but be transformed by the renewing of your mind, that you may prove what is that good and acceptable and perfect will of God" Romans 12:1-2, NKJV.

There's nothing quick or painless about the Cross, and Jesus demands getting on it daily. A surrendered sacrifice is the only sacrifice God will accept. The nails did not hold Jesus on the Cross, the task at hand did. The nails will not hold us on the Cross, only a life submitted to Jesus will keep our flesh where it belongs, humble and yielded to Him.

"Then He said to them all, "If anyone desires to come after Me, let him deny himself, and take up his cross daily, and follow Me" Luke 9:23, NKJV.

We could look at many men and women of Scripture that lived this crucified life, and please understand we are not talking about a perfect life. No one I know believes in sinless perfection, our flesh must be conquered, and it truly is a daily battle. In his letter to the Galatians, Paul tells us of our flesh warring against our spirit and our spirit warring against the flesh. Our flesh is not the same as our spirit, and Paul tells us in Romans chapter eight that we are still waiting for the redemption of our bodies.

"For we know that the whole creation groans and labors with birth pangs together until now. Not only that, but we also who have the firstfruits of the Spirit, even we ourselves groan within ourselves, eagerly waiting for the adoption, the redemption of our body" Romans 8:22-23, NKJV.

Our bodies will die because of sin, and we must crucify it every day until it finally does, releasing our spirits to return to Abba. To be absent from the body is to be present with The Lord, Scripture tells us. I doubt this will ever be a popular message, but one very necessary in the day we live. Gross darkness is covering the land and dear saints of God, we must *arise and shine* as lights. America needs awakening, the world needs revival, and it will not come upon a people of darkness until the people of light separate themselves unto The King. My flesh, your flesh, our flesh wars against this surrender but beloved of The Lord, it is essential.

I mentioned earlier we could talk of many saints that led this type of life, martyrs in Scripture and out but today, I want to talk to you about someone you may have never thought of in this light. The young man I am writing about is found in the book of beginnings.

"Now it came to pass after these things that God tested Abraham, and said to him, "Abraham!" And he said, "Here I am." Then He said, "Take now your son, your only son Isaac, whom you love, and go to the

land of Moriah, and offer him there as a burnt offering on one of the mountains of which I shall tell you" Genesis 22:1-2, NKJV.

Despite his flaws, it is no wonder Abraham is called the *father of faith*. The Bible tells us early the next morning, Abraham saddled his animal, gathered the wood for the sacrifice, gathered his son and young men, and headed out. He did not wait for two months to make sure he heard the voice of God. We need to live lives where we fear hearing God and refusing to obey more than we fear missing Him and inconveniencing our lives; you should probably read that again.

"Then they came to the place of which God had told him. And Abraham built an altar there and placed the wood in order; and he bound Isaac his son and laid him on the altar, upon the wood. And Abraham stretched out his hand and took the knife to slay his so" Genesis 22:9, NKJV.

We have heard this account unfold countless times and generally the talk is about Abraham, and rightly so. The Bible tells us much more about him than Isaac's response to this event. I believe the lack of text concerning Isaac speaks volumes. The Bible has never hid the flaws of God's servants. We know about David's sins, Peter's denial, Paul's strong will, and Thomas' doubt. The Bible tells us so much about the flaws of the people of God; if we have spent the time studying it, our hearts are comforted knowing God doesn't need perfect people to work through. Peter goes from denying Jesus in His most critical hour to standing before thousands and rebuking them harshly for the wickedness they committed against God's Son and three thousand were saved in a single service! God uses imperfect people of which I am the one, maybe the least perfect of all!

Scripture gives no clue of flaw in Isaac in this instance. Abraham bound him and placed him on the altar without a mention of any struggle. Isaac lay there waiting for the knife to come from the hand of his father. We tend to think Isaac was a child when this event took place, and we do not know for certain, but Jewish scholars believe he was between twenty-six and thirty-seven years old. I wouldn't be surprised to find out when we get to Heaven he was thirty-three and a half. Let's just say he was thirty, Abraham would be one hundred thirty, and seeing he lived to be one hundred seventy-five, it would not be strange he still had strength enough to lift Isaac to the altar.

Think about it, if Isaac was indeed thirty, he could have fought off his father, he could have resisted what he had to see unfolding before his eyes, but he submitted to the sacrifice.

Yes, Abraham learned what it was like to lay his son upon the altar of sacrifice as did his heavenly Father before the foundation of the world. God knew what it was like to give up His One and Only Son, and so He set precedent in the early days of faith that was to come to save the world. Salvation comes through sacrifice; Abraham knew firsthand what it felt like to lay his one and only seed of Promise on the altar, as Father knew as well. The main point here today is Isaac knew what it was like to be laid on that altar to be the sacrifice.

Isaac laid his life down because he trusted his father. My dear friend, you can lay your life down because your Father can be trusted! Isaac fulfilled his mission from God, he didn't die on the altar that day, and though we lay our life down on our cross, we don't die, we come alive.

"And do not be conformed to this world, but be transformed by the renewing of your mind, that you may prove what is that good and acceptable and perfect will of God" Romans 12:2, NKJV.

I believe the only way to know how good and perfect and pleasing the will of God is, is to live the crucified life!

Paul declared:

"I have been crucified with Christ; it is no longer I who live, but Christ lives in me; and the life which I now live in the flesh I live by faith in the Son of God, who loved me and gave Himself for me" Galatians 2:20, NKJV.

Christ lives in me!!! What is a more powerful declaration than that?

Go ahead my dear friend, lay that life down, lay on the altar of sacrifice as Isaac did, and stop fighting your Father. If you must fight, fight down that flesh that keeps demanding its way. The less of us in charge, the more we will see Jesus living and moving through our lives.

Pray this prayer with me: Father, Your Kingdom come, Your will be done in my life. I surrender to Your will, I surrender to Your grace. Father, do whatever You must to bring me to the place of total surrender, total submission, in Jesus' Name, Amen!

Ananias

Rich Miller

"I was blinded by the intense light and had to be led by the hand to Damascus by my companions. A man named Ananias lived there. He was a godly man, deeply devoted to the law, and well regarded by all the Jews of Damascus." Acts 22:11-12

As a man, I like to think of myself as bold and courageous. The protector and provider of the family. Not intimidated by the challenges that life may throw my way. Never letting thoughts of fear limit me or those that follow me from stepping into all that God has planned for us. But am I really? Do I recklessly obey the Voice of the Lord without any restraint? I think we all can use a reminder now and then of the goodness of God. I know that I can. How soon we can forget that *while we were still sinners, Christ died for us.* While we were deserving of death, Christ died in our place. He never looked over at the Father and said, "But I have heard what this man has been doing. Are you sure I should do this? Is this really going to turn out like you say?" Jesus did not let my behavior influence His obedience to the Voice of the Father. Neither did He let a desire for His own comfort stop Him from following through.

Maybe this is true of you as well. But not for me. I have rationalized the risks associated with obeying the Voice of the Lord. I have reasoned sometimes that what God has said to me doesn't make logical sense. I have feared what could happen if it didn't go as planned. I have wondered if I was really hearing correctly since what I felt in my spirit didn't line up with what I saw with my eyes. The late John Wimber said that faith is spelled R-I-S-K. He was right.

In Acts chapter 9, we get introduced to a man named Ananias. According to the Apostle Paul, *he was a godly man, deeply devoted to the law, and well regarded by all the Jews of Damascus*. This story and the testimony of it written in Acts 22 are the only times that he is mentioned. But what an impact he made.

"The Lord said, "Go over to Straight Street, to the house of Judas. When you get there, ask for a man from Tarsus named Saul. He is praying to me right now. I have shown him a vision of a man named Ananias coming in and laying hands on him so he can see again" Acts 9:11–12, NLT.

In these verses, we get a glimpse into the multi-tasking of God. While Saul is praying, God shows him a vision of Ananias coming to heal his blindness and at the same time, He is giving the instructions to Ananias in a separate vision. This is quite a display of God's wisdom and power. I think we all have a desire for more of this! But it is in Ananias's response is where I sometimes find myself.

"But Lord," exclaimed Ananias, "I've heard many people talk about the terrible things this man has done to the believers in Jerusalem! And he is authorized by the leading priests to arrest everyone who calls upon your name" Acts 9:13–14, NLT.

In my opinion, as the command of the Lord soaked in, Ananias wrestled with two thoughts:
1. Saul's sins
2. Ananias's safety

He didn't want to go. It seemed dangerous to him. But the Lord said to him, *"Go, for he is a chosen vessel of Mine to bear My name before Gentiles, kings, and the children of Israel"* Acts 9:15, NKJV. The story goes on in verse 17 with Ananias obeying the Lord and doing exactly what He had said. The rest is history. I find comfort in the fact that Ananias struggled with his assignment. It's good to know that I am not the only one. But Paul's testimony of this in Acts 22 sheds even more light on how impactful this encounter was for him.

"I was blinded by the intense light and had to be led by the hand to Damascus by my companions. A man named Ananias lived there. He was a godly man, deeply devoted to the law, and well regarded by all the Jews of Damascus. He came and stood beside me and said, 'Brother Saul, regain your sight.' And that very moment I could see him! "Then he told me, 'The God of our ancestors has chosen you to know his will and to see the Righteous One and hear him speak. For you are to be his witness, telling everyone what you have seen and heard. What are you waiting for? Get up and be baptized. Have your sins washed away by calling on the name of the Lord'"* Acts 22:11–16, NLT.

Three things jump out at me from Paul's testimony.

1. Ananias came and stood by him.

I believe this is one of the most powerful statements in the story of Ananias. I don't think it is by chance that Paul mentions Ananias *came and stood by him*. This was a defining moment for Saul. Saul was normally the one standing by someone else. He stood with those who stoned Stephen. He was beyond confident. But now, Saul needed someone to stand by him. Other than Paul's testimony, we never hear of Ananias again. Presumably, his life would have been the same whether he went or not. His obedience was not about him. But for Paul, it was a moment he would never forget, when a man named Ananias stood by him. It was as if his life was suspended in time, waiting for this essential encounter to launch him into the rest of his life. For Ananias, it was an elective. Basically, a nonessential. For Paul, it was a pivotal moment in his life.

It is no different for us. It really has nothing to do with us. It is not because we are so wise. God has chosen to use people like you and me to bring understanding to what is in another person's heart. Sometimes, what people need is for someone to come along and stand by them. That is what Paul remembered. The world will remember that we stood by them, regardless of their past.

2. Ananias said to Paul. "Regain your sight."

Ananias took a risk. Beyond the risk of meeting up with Saul! Yes, that was a risk, a huge risk. But he laid his hands on the guy! And then commanded him to see. What if that didn't work? You know that is exactly what was running through Ananias's mind. Oh, we think that people in the Bible didn't think those kinds of thoughts. But they did. Ananias was taking thoughts of fear captive and casting down arguments long before Paul ever instructed the Corinthian church to do so in 2 Corinthians10:5. He pushed past every bit of intimidation that was telling him this wasn't a good idea.

This was not the safe route. This was out of his comfort zone. He wrestled with his thoughts, his emotions, his doubts and fears just like we would. It is easy for us to look at this as a success story. But from the other side, this would have looked like it could end badly. All of our challenges look more intimidating beforehand than after. Just like Ananias, I have had said, "BUT LORD" when the Lord has asked me to do things outside of my comfort zone. Ananias took a risk and Saul received a miracle. His blind eyes were opened. I cannot let my desire for comfort and safety keep people from their miracle. God give me the courage of Ananias.

3. Ananias told Paul what God was saying about him.

Sometimes, the things that God places on our heart are not comfortable. Maybe they are even unreasonable in our minds. When God says, "Go find the guy you are hiding from, the one who wants to arrest you, and give him a message from me," we have our reservations. For Ananias, the reputation of Saul is easily seen. This guy was making the headlines. For us, sometimes it just doesn't add up in our minds. We may not know the person that well. Or maybe we know them too well. Maybe, the message doesn't sound logical to us. Or it doesn't fit with what we know about the person.

This reminds me of one of my favorite lines from the Book of Daniel. In Daniel 2:30 (NLT), Daniel says to King Nebuchadnezzar, "...

it is not because I am wiser than anyone else that I know the secret of your dream, but because God wants you to understand what was in your heart."

Just like God was using Daniel to get information to the King, God was using Ananias to get information to Saul. God's message was the opposite of what things looked like in the natural. From Ananias's perspective, Saul was a spokesperson for the devil, not a witness for Jesus. But Ananias was able to remove all preconceived ideas and prejudices about Saul and just deliver the message. That is our job. It is not *our* message. It is a message from God to the other person. We are just servants and stewards of the message.

A man unrestrained...
When I read the story of Ananias, I see a man I can relate to. He questioned what God told him to do. He was uncertain about the calling on Saul based on his reputation. Is meeting with him really safe? What will people say about me meeting with him? We all have our questions. Our concerns. Our pleas to stay within the boundaries of our comfort zone. But Ananias pushed past those things. He destroyed every restraint that tried to keep him from delivering the message. He demonstrated the love of God to a man that hated Christians. He showed the power of God by opening the blind eyes of a man he was hoping wouldn't find him and possibly arrest or kill him. And he announced the purpose of God by delivering the Word of the Lord to Saul. Because of the obedience of Ananias to go and deliver the message God had given him, the world is not the same.

My prayer for us, for men, is that we would be unrestrained by fear and intimidation like Ananias. That we would be free from our comfort zones to be used by God to shift the life of another person and change their world forever.

Abraham

Jeff Linzay

"No longer shall your name be called Abram, but your name shall be Abraham; for I have made you a father of many nations." Genesis 17:5

The Lord tells Abram at the age of seventy-five to *gather your family and your belongings and leave your home.* Go to a place I will show you and I will make you a great nation. Abram and his wife have no children, but he does as the Lord instructed him. Abram obeys and leaves to go to the place the Lord will show him. He takes his wife, his nephew Lot, and all his possessions. There will be times in every believer's life, like Abram's, when the Lord will say to leave what you were called to last season and are comfortable doing to accomplish His will in the next season, in the place He will show us.

When a man of God shifts seasons and positions with the Lord, he will alter the lives of all those attached to him. He not only changes his position and life in the Kingdom, but also changes the course of his family for future generations. This is an honor as head of a household, but also a great responsibility. The Word of God says in Samuel 15: 21-23, *"Obedience to the Lord births a blessing, but disobedience is as the sin of witchcraft."* Like Abraham, we must pursue obedience and purpose to establish blessings from our Lord for ourselves and future generations.

During a meeting to call a pastor to a church my family had been a part of for many years, the Lord told me that my season at this church was over. The next thing He said was *get your things and leave now*. I gathered my Bible and paperwork and quietly walked out the back of the room. We had been a part of this body for many years and very actively involved. Our community of close friends were all tied to this church. All of this changed in a day. We became outsiders in a day. I didn't understand the season, but I knew clearly I had heard the voice of the Lord and I obeyed. Soon, I met a local minister and went to his church to honor him. I told the Lord I wasn't getting involved in anything. I just wanted to sit in the back, listen to the Word, and leave. I believe the Lord laughs in Heaven when we declare our plans without consulting Him. Within a few weeks, the Lord instructed me to begin interceding for the Pastor. I reluctantly agreed and set in motion my ministry path for the next decade and a half. I would sit outside the Pastor's office and intercede before every service.

Shortly thereafter, the Pastor and I began to pray together before every service. This began a season where men would gather together to pray and seek the Lord before every service. We had one goal, to seek Jesus to see His will be done in people's lives, including our own. Our goal was to introduce people to our risen Savior, Jesus. To get their hands and lives firmly in the hands of Jesus, and then get out of the way. My prayer was that they would see and receive from Jesus and not man. The power of these prayer groups was incredible! The Holy Spirit always honored our prayer time and displayed His glory and power. It was often difficult to stand as we would gather in a circle holding hands praying for the congregation, each other, and the will of the Lord to be done. The power of God was so strong that after many prayer times, no one would be left standing. As the power of the Lord's presence occurred, healings, answered prayers, and demonstrations of the Lord's power were present. As we prayed in the Pastor's office, the same power and glory of the Lord's presence was happening in the sanctuary. The power of the Lord's presence was glorious and signs and wonders were occurring regularly.

We experienced many miraculous encounters and visitations. One Sunday morning, while praying with the Pastor, I saw a hand coming toward me and it made me step back. It was not a hand in the natural and it was headed toward the Pastor. I shared what I was seeing with the Pastor and he began to weep loudly. He had just been diagnosed with cancer and had asked the Lord for a hug that morning in his personal prayer time. When we would exit from our prayer time, the power of God would visibly touch and impact people we would pass in the hallway and in the sanctuary. It was a great season with the Lord. I was the intercessor for the Pastor and was able to travel for ministry. We traveled extensively throughout the United States and other countries ministering. He was also my closest friend. I was ordained and able to pray and minister to his bride. What an honor to serve the Body of Christ.

One Sunday morning, after entering into the worship service, I was kneeling down during worship time. The Lord asked me, "Will you leave when I tell you?" I hesitated, not wanting to answer. I did not reply and the Lord asked me again sternly, "Will you leave when I tell you?" I replied with tears streaming down my cheeks, *yes Lord*, fully expecting to hear *take up your things and leave*. He did not tell me to leave that day, but He did rebuke me saying, *this is His Kingdom and He is the King*. The Lord said to me He alone is to be worshipped and we must obey His voice over every other voice. So, the Lord began to prepare me to leave even though the actual departure would occur years later. The Lord will allow situations to occur to facilitate His plans for our lives. Things were very good at the church and I didn't think I would ever leave. The Lord was nudging me to leave and I was resistant. Then, the rejection came as the prayer times were cancelled by the Pastor. The body shifted from being led by prayer to boards and committees. I did not want to leave and uproot my family after years of fellowship and serving for almost two decades.

The Lord had shown me that once I left, I would not be able to go back. He even sent one of the elders to tell me the Lord had shown him the one who was closest to me in the Body would put his arm around me and shove a knife into my ribs. The attack was spiritual and not physical. The Lord also sent prophetic voices that spoke to us privately in the pastor's office saying they have turned against you. Yet, I was resistant to leave. The certainty of misery is sometimes more comfortable than the misery of uncertainty.

As spiritual leader of my family, I should have spent more time in prayer, asking the Lord to reveal His timing and guidance. Finally, I got a call from a close friend and a powerful minister. They asked if I would do them a favor. I said that I would, if I was able. They made me promise to do the favor and that I would be able. Being a dear friend and trusted voice in my life, I agreed. They asked me to leave and never go back to the church, that it was not healthy for me or my family. I kept my promise and left. It was very painful and began a season of perceived isolation and rejection. It was an unwritten but clearly expressed law that if you left this Body, you were in rebellion and would be excommunicated by all the members. This was a difficult and painful season for my family and me. I have always tried to be led by the Holy Spirit and not driven by circumstances. This is no excuse as a leader not to ask for an Issachar anointing and to gain discernment over the times and seasons for our personal lives. Honestly, I avoided the subject because I was comfortable and caused my family to endure a lot of abuse and suffering due to my disobedience. I can only blame myself for this season, regardless of the actions of others.

The Lord never left nor forsook my family or me. He has drawn me and my family to Him closer than ever before. What feels like rejection and isolation to the flesh is often consecration to the Lord. If we will draw close to Him, He will draw close to us. If we seek the Lord, He will be found. If we honor Him, He will stay. If the Lord stays, He will do what His Word and voice declares. The Lord has allowed me to fellowship with incredible ministries and ministers. I have been ordained by a powerful and precious minister of Jesus Christ. Thank you, Jason Beard, for your faith and trust in ordaining and commissioning me to go forth declaring the Gospel, saving the lost, and setting the captives free in the mighty name of Jesus.

In Genesis 26:5, the Lord states Abraham and his descendants will be blessed because Abraham obeyed the Lord, did everything the Lord requested, and kept his commands, decrees, and instructions. Simply put, faithful obedience births blessings that are generational. I implore you, love and obey the Lord in every area, so that generational blessings will occur in Jesus' name. The line between righteousness and rebellion is often much smaller than we think and can only be discerned and guided by the voice of God. The beauty of Jesus is that His mercies are new every morning and we can start each day with the ability to bring glory and honor to His name and Kingdom. God alone owns our destiny. We will be wounded and offended at times. If we pick up offenses, then we will have to carry them, until we forgive and lay them down at the foot of the Cross. The weight of carrying offenses will keep us wounded and bound until we release them and lay them down. If we continue to carry offense, it will limit our growth, our fellowship with believers and Yeshua, and limit our destiny in Christ. We serve a limitless God. The only thing that will limit Him in our lives, is our unbelief and disobedience.

Many times, like with Abraham, much time passes between the promise of God and the manifestation of that promise. We must rest assured that when God said it, it is done! If we become impatient and do not wait upon the Lord, we may produce an Ishmael, instead of an Isaac. The very calling of God commissioned and ordained by God for our lives, outside the timing of God, is outside the will of God. Our destiny rests in and is fashioned by our limitless Father and the resurrected Jesus we serve. We do not have to wonder what the will of God is for us or those around us. His Word says that He desires that all should be saved and that none should perish, 2 Peter 3:9. The Lord is the righteous judge; Jesus and His blood declares our innocence and the Holy Spirit is our advocate. He also says He will give us the ability to pray the mysteries of Heaven. The Lord has prepared the system in such a way that the only way for us to lose is by rejecting the sacrifice and saving grace of Jesus. Jesus' shed blood, death, burial, and resurrection have provided a pathway for restored fellowship with our Lord where we are covered by an eternal blood covenant with the King of kings and the Lord of lords. We have the calling and ability to walk in covenant with Jesus and the Father by the guidance of the Holy Spirit. This comes with eternal blessings but also incredible responsibilities to walk in obedience.

Destiny cannot be seen, but must be visualized. Destiny cannot be grasped, but must be embraced. Destiny cannot be located, but must be stepped into. May Yeshua's love, power, and grace fill each of us. Father, we ask that You release the Ruach (breath of God) to us and fill us with Your presence and destiny. Father, we ask that Your power transition all those attached to us into Your will and destiny as we follow You. I encourage each of you to step into your destiny in Christ, Amen.

Mephibosheth

Mike Hendrick

"Jonathan, Saul's son, had a son who was lame in his feet. He was five years old when the news about Saul and Jonathan came from Jezreel; and his nurse took him up and fled. And it happened, as she made haste to flee, that he fell and became lame. His name was Mephibosheth." 1 Kings 17:1

Back in June of 2023, I was invited by my friend John Kurish, a minister, to visit the Durham region of Ontario. The Durham Region is at the apex of much of the automotive manufacturing industry in Canada and the 401 Corridor that stretches from Oshawa, Ontario to the outskirts of Toronto. It has been a manufacturing hub for many years in Canada. While on that trip, John had asked me to speak to a men's recovery ministry that his church helps to support. Whenever I get an opportunity to encourage people, I take time to prepare myself to hear what the Lord would have me speak about. As I got quiet before the Lord, I felt Him say, "Son, I would like you to speak on the topic of identity and how it pertains to rejection." My message for the men at the recovery center was going to be about two men in the Bible who had identity issues that contributed to their battle with rejection in life, Mephibosheth and Bartimaeus, and how they dealt with the rejections of their lives. In this devotional, I would like to highlight *Mephibosheth*.

While crossing the street on my way to speak, I rolled and fractured my right ankle. Instant pain shot through my right leg. I heard the sound of my right ankle bone snapping. Now, you may be asking the question, what does a fractured leg have to do with identity? A fracture in the leg will cause a person to limp unless an individual gets it treated. A fractured identity will create a limp in an individual's journey of life unless healed and will influence and shape the inner and outer worlds of individuals dealing with rejection. To heal from an ankle fracture, an orthopedic doctor will put an individual in an air cast or cast for several weeks to immobilize the ankle, allowing the bone to fuse and heal. Depending on the severity of the fracture, they may even perform surgery on your ankle, putting pins and screws in the ankle to reset the bone. They put the cast on the broken limb to prevent movement. Typically, the fracture takes six weeks to heal and movement can begin again. This isn't always the case as more severe fractures can take longer to heal. It is up to the cooperation and willingness between patient and doctor that helps heal the fracture.

If we are dealing with a fractured identity in our life and desire to heal; sometimes, we must have a time out where we spend some time with a registered psychologist or counsellor walking through the entanglements of our lives. With their skilled precision, a counsellor or psychologist can immobilize rejection, putting it in a safe cast of protection. They can assist to unravel and discern the events in our lives that contributed to rejection that influence our identity. This will enable our rejection wound to begin healing, while displacing a false identity and assume our true identity. It may take a while to deal with the entanglements of rejection as more than likely, it contributed to how we survived in the world. Over time, and with submission, the wounds of a fractured identity can heal and like an ankle fracture, you may still feel the effects of it in your walk even as you heal.

Our families of origin contribute to the formation of our identities. From an early age, we learn behavior patterns that establish our personalities, self-worth, and identities. We learn a lot about how to behave through how our siblings and parents treat us. It was God's intent from the beginning that the family would be a safe place of acceptance, free from rejection. However, due to sin and the brokenness of the family, rejection is far too common in families. Siblings compete for the love and acceptance of parents and compare themselves to each other, sometimes devastating the sibling with a weaker sense of identity. Siblings will compare themselves in various ways: athletic ability, academic performance, physical stature, intelligence, even in jobs or careers, and a wide variety of other areas. All of this can be a breeding ground for rejection. If a sibling does not feel they can measure up to the other siblings and the parents do not adjust it with nurture and love, the sibling can take on a rejection complex. Even parents can unknowingly contribute to the rejection in the development of their child. It can result from a parent's own insecurity of the child, an inability to bond with the child, or the personal struggles a child has in their development. It could also be many other areas such as performance in school or activities. Children derive a lot of their identity from both parents and siblings and when there is a fracture in that, it can contribute a lot to rejection developing in their personality.

Mephibosheth was the grandson of Saul, the first king of Israel. Mephibosheth was the son of Jonathan. His name in Hebrew means "From the Mouth of Shame." Jonathan was one of Saul's sons who was slain in battle against the Philistine army but was a friend of David, the son of Jessie and successor to King Saul. David and Jonathan had a special covenantal relationship of peace with each other that if anything would happen to either party, the other would ensure kindness and protection to the other party's family. Jonathan's father, King Saul, had been pursuing David and because of his jealous insecurity, wanted to murder David. Jonathan loved David as a brother and because of the love each of them had for one another as friends, they promised each other that they would show kindness to the other's descendants. In Biblical times, covenant was taken seriously. Not only that, if a king was killed by a party, the entire family would be killed off, thus preventing a future insurrection by the family.

Mephibosheth was five years old when Jonathan and Saul were slain in battle. Mephibosheth had a nursing attendant who ran when she heard the news that Jonathan and Saul had died in battle. She left in such a hurry that either Mephibosheth fell, or was dropped, leaving him crippled. This event had a profound impact on Mephibosheth's development.

Not only did his father and grandfather die the same day, but he also had to go into hiding. The very family that gave him identity was gone in a moment and he would grow up knowing that at any moment, he could be killed if anyone found out he was a family descendent of King Saul. When he was dropped, Mephibosheth was crippled and more than likely was seeking out a life knowing he had come from a lineage of kingship. But he also knew that his grandfather Saul had been rejected as king by God. All of this culminated in a shame-riddled, rejection-filled life with no hope of anything better to come, and living way below what he felt he would have had should his father and grandfather still be alive. That is until years later, David remembered his promise that he had made Jonathan. One day, David was talking with a servant of Saul's family wondering if there was any member of Saul's family still alive that he could show kindness. The servant told him about Mephibosheth still living, in a place in Israel called Lo Debar, a barren ghetto town. David instantly called for Mephibosheth. Not knowing what to expect, Mephibosheth came cautiously to David's palace, more than likely in fear of his life and probably expecting more rejection. Little did he know that day would change the rest of his life and deal a blow to the rejection that had enshrined his identity.

Upon arriving at the palace, Mephibosheth was escorted to David's room where David warmly greeted him. Instead of being treated like an enemy, Mephibosheth was treated as family and was invited to eat at the king's table as one of the sons of the King. Mephibosheth's deep rejection was expressed in his response to David's offer, asking David why a *dead dog* like him would be given such an honor. David told Mephibosheth that it was because of his promise to Jonathan that Mephibosheth got all of Saul's lands, all that belonged to Saul, back and was going to eat at the king's table for the rest of his life. He was given a new place to live in Jerusalem, never having to return to Lo Debar again, and even had servants who would till the land and provide for him and his family. What is interesting is that there is no mention that Mephibosheth ever called himself a *dead dog*, a derogatory term of rejection, again. He was still crippled but the rejection had been displaced in his life. His name also can mean *Shame Destroyer* or *Image Breaker*, which can show us today that God can transform and heal our entire identity, changing how we view ourselves, and displace rejection.

That, my friends, is what Jesus does for us. He transforms our identity and removes the stigma of rejection from our heart. Earlier, I mentioned the Hebrew word "Tov." When we were declared "Tov" by God at the beginning, it had everything to do with our identity as people. The word implies a complete validation; it serves the function it was designed and created for, much like a well-oiled machine. It shows the power of something, or someone, fulfilling a divine purpose and being actively engaged in the process. It is a bringing forth of God's purpose and identity in a person. So, let me ask, does Tov have anything to do with our outward performance, validation, and acceptance, or is it just bestowed upon us? I believe it is bestowed us by God. It is He who completely validates us as Creator, and it is He who approves and accepts us fully as we were created by Him, in His image, as His sons and daughters, which should establish our identity. Sure, God uses humans to reinforce others' identities, but when we are secure in our identity as His first, everything else settles.

One excellent resource on this topic is a book written by Rosaria Butterfield entitled: *"The Secret Thoughts of an Unlikely Convert: An English Professor's Journey into the Christian Faith."* In this book, Butterfield explores her journey to faith in Christ through an unlikely friendship that developed with Ken Smith, an evangelistic Christian. Butterfield was an openly lesbian activist who wrote an article against the religious right and politics of hatred only to find her own beliefs challenged when she met and became friends with Smith and his wife. This culminated in her re-examining her own beliefs and finding Christ during her journey.

I, too, need the Grace of God in my own brokenness and my identity. I struggled with so much brokenness in my own journey. I did not know who I was when I was younger. The years of peer abuse left me questioning my value and the rejection of many young women in my life made me wonder who would ever want to love me. It was a real battle of knowing that I was loved. A self-righteous, holier than thou approach never works in trying to influence people in their struggles. Why not take the approach of, *come with me on a journey into my own broken life and I will show you my struggles, temptations, and vices*? We all have them. To be ignorant of them is to be ignorant of what we all face daily.

In my own life, I struggled with my own identity issues. I am not immune to identity struggles. When I was younger, I was the target of bullying and abuse by peers, which contributed to a fractured identity. I was physically smaller than a lot of my peers, I was not athletic, and I was a slow learner. All of this contributed to a false and fractured sense of identity in my internal world. One of the other major factors was being sexually abused two or three times by three young men. It affected me so greatly that I could not easily connect with men for most of my life. I did not realize until getting professional counselling that my male issues stemmed from the abuse from my peers years earlier, which also contributed to a deep fracture in my male identity. I was always a soft-spoken individual and overly submissive. This engrained a deep timidity and insecurity in my personality. I never wanted to rock the boat and in turn, people pleased to get my sense of acceptance and identity. I had such a fractured sense of identity that if people disagreed with me, I interpreted it as rejection of myself and felt worthless. I did not realize that my wounded personality was contributing to my rejection.

When going through my own inner healing process, I was able to see that there were subconscious behaviors that made people feel uneasy around me. Nervous behaviors had been established in my personality, which manifested externally in my life. Unknowingly, I had caused my own rejection by these nervous behaviors that had taken root in my life. Through the help of a trusted counsellor, I have started to recognize these subconscious behaviors and remove them from my life. I am not there fully yet as I am still healing but each day, I find myself more and more victorious.

For those who struggle with identity issues, I would suggest finding a trusted psychologist or counsellor that can help you untangle the lies of identity that you have believed. It is not an easy process but the more you heal, the more you will be able to express a healthy self-identity and walk free from the entanglements of a confused, fractured identity into a victorious understanding of who you are as a loved son or daughter of a loving Heavenly Father.

Noah

Randy H. Davis

"But Noah found grace in the eyes of the Lord." Genesis 6:8

God called Noah to perform a specific job. He was beyond frustrated with what His Creation had become. Genesis 6:1-6 describes how God felt about what He saw when He looked at Creation. *"And it repented the Lord that He had made man on the earth, and it grieved Him at His heart."* The wickedness reached such a level that God repented, was sorry, that He had created man. In His sorrow over the wickedness of His Creation, God looked and saw Noah, and Noah found grace in the eyes of God, Genesis 6:8.

In a corrupt and wicked world, the life of Noah stood out as one that did not reflect the wickedness of the rest of the world. Note that Noah was not performing miracles. Noah was not preaching eloquent sermons. *Noah walked with God.* The way Noah lived his life day to day amidst the wickedness that filled the world caused Noah to find grace in the eyes of the Lord. Nineveh was on God's radar and benefited because God wanted to change Jonah's heart. Sodom and Gomorrah's sin cried out to God, so that He sent angels in to see how bad it really was, and they proved themselves by their actions. The wickedness of man was so great that God repented, was sorry, that He had made man in the Earth. When everything around Noah was as bad as it could get, Noah chose to live in a manner that pleased God. There is no note or mention that Noah looked around and saw how bad things were, saw the wickedness of man, and decided he was going to audition for God's favor. Noah chose to live for God amidst all the wickedness of man. Because Noah loved God and sought to please God with his life, he stood out to God, not because He was less wicked than the rest of humanity. He was not the lesser of several evils. *Noah walked with God.* The life Noah lived was a result of how he chose to be, not what he decided to do. A just man and perfect in his generation spoke to who Noah was as a man. A "just" man, from the Hebrew word tsaddiyq, (*tsad-deek'*) meaning *lawful or righteous*. So, when the world around him was wicked, he was lawful and righteous. Lawful and righteous means not only was he lawful and righteous according to the law of the land, but also before the Lord. In addition to being known a just man, he was said to be "perfect". Perfect in the Hebrew is tamiym (*taw-meem'*) meaning *entire, complete, whole, sound, or undefiled.* So, Noah found grace in God's eye because of the life he chose to live before the Lord.

Standing out amidst all man's wickedness made Noah and his family worthy to be the filter through which God would purge the wickedness from humanity. Humanity had demonstrated they were worthy of destruction before God. Nineveh was warned of destruction. Sodom and Gomorrah brough destruction upon themselves. Humanity was so wicked that it needed a purging, a filtering, and Noah, by being a just man and perfect in his generation, walked with God and put himself in position to be that filter without even knowing it. Noah's honorable life caused him to be chosen and tasked with building the ark. The ark would be the vessel that God used to preserve, to transport life from the wickedness of man to a fresh new world purged of man's rampant wickedness. Noah ties into the person of Jesus in that just as man's wickedness was purged from humanity through the filter of Noah (the Ark), so, too, was humanity saved and cleansed by the blood of Jesus on the Cross.

The Bible also mentions another characteristic of Noah that pleased God, and that was *obedience*. Genesis 6:22 says, *"Thus did Noah, according to all that God had commanded him, so did he."* So, along with his other character strengths, Noah was obedient. The ark took 55-75 years to build, proving that Noah was also persistent, persevering, and enduring. Do I believe that my life stands out so magnificently from the wickedness in the world that God would pick me out to carry out such a task? No. Do I see myself as someone through whom God could filter all humanity and do a semi-reboot? No, neither did Noah. I will say that if a person is willing to live their life in accordance with God's Word and submit to His will for their lives, they open themselves up to be used by God in similar fashion. The most significant thing that could be said of Noah is in Genesis 6:b, "...and Noah walked with God."

God chose me to undertake a task that required obedience, faith, endurance, and persistence. Noah was asked to build the 750 feet long, forty-five feet wide, and thirty-five feet high ark. He did not live next to a body of water that justified such a vessel being built. Nothing about the situation justified Noah building the ark, nothing to the naked eye, nothing to anyone that was not named *Noah*. He must have faced ridicule from those who learned what he was doing. He had to have fielded questions about what he was doing. Noah built the ark. No one came to offer Noah assistance; the mission and the purpose did not make enough sense for anyone to believe Noah needed help building this folly. Noah built the ark. When it was finished, God brought the animals to Noah and in the designated numbers for what He had commanded. They all boarded the ark and God closed the door.

On March 6, 2011, my wife and I planted a church in Las Vegas, Nevada. We had been planted in a church by God and we enjoyed worshipping and serving there. We watched that church decline, split, and die. I was asked to serve as interim pastor of one of the sides of the split and I agreed to with the intent of bringing about a reconciliation between the previous pastor and the congregants of both sides of the split. That did not happen. Eventually, a permanent pastor was appointed, and our side of the split died. As I was praying about how to keep the "baby" alive, God spoke to me clearly through yet another pastor and his words were, *"the baby is dead."* He was referring to the situation between David and Bathsheba where the son they had was sick and finally died. God was letting me know that I did not have to be concerned with how to try to keep this side of the split alive. *The baby was dead.*

I spent the next few months praying about what to do, and where to go to worship God. We had to be a part of a local body. I had heard from different people that we should just start a church, but that was never a part of the plan. After more prayer, God let me know that this was now a part of the plan. So, on March 6, 2011, we started a new church. My wife stood with me and ministered alongside me in different capacities over the next several years. God used our ruddy little ministry to do some great things and touch numerous lives along the way. We did homeless outreach and had dynamic women's crusades. All the while, we never had more than a handful of faithful members. Sometimes, our numbers in service were just the six of us: me, my wife, and our four boys. I even preached one Sunday to empty chairs when my family was out of town and our other member were out. On days when it was just us, a feeling of defeat would try to set in. I would stand before my family and say, "We're on the ark today." Then, I would remind them that only Noah and his family made it to the ark.

The account of Noah building the ark hit home with us numerous times during our eleven years in Las Vegas. It was seventeen years in total, but eleven as our *ruddy little church*. I say "ruddy little church" because that is how David was described in the Bible. He was small but good to look at. Our numbers were few, but I know that when God looked at us, He was pleased at what He saw, how He always found us. It took Noah-like persistence and perseverance to keep building that ark. It took knowing that God had purposed by calling us to this task of giving people the opportunity to come experience Him in worship. We were blessed, randomly by our sight, purposefully by God's plan, many different times over the years.

The church started in our home but we moved to the meeting room of a local hotel. While we were in the hotel meeting room, a young man from Chino, California joined us. He proceeded to tell us his testimony of how he got saved. He also spoke encouraging words to us that only God could have given him to speak. Another time we were in worship and three teenagers joined us, two young women and a young man. They sat down and the young man immediately fell to his knees and began praying and worshipping right there on the spot. They had to leave before service was over and when they realized they had to go, it was clear that they were not ready to leave that atmosphere.

We spent much of our time in Las Vegas building an ark. We have merged that ministry God allowed us to lead with another ministry that needed help, here in my hometown of Galesburg, Illinois. We have endured years of building, persevering, persisting, and enduring knowing only that God had called us out to a task. We do not know when the rain will come, all we know is that we must keep building.

It took Noah between 55 and 75 years to build the ark. He knew God would not send the flood before the ark was complete. If you are building an ark, the rain floods are coming, but God will not send it until the ark is finished. Keep building!

Aaron

F. Shadrach Oloo

"So the anger of the Lord was kindled against Moses, and He said: "Is not Aaron the Levite your brother? I know that he can speak well. And look, he is also coming out to meet you. When he sees you, he will be glad in his heart." Exodus 4:14

The renowned leadership author and trainer, John Maxwell, says that "everything stands or falls on leadership". There are many lessons we, especially men, can learn from the person of Aaron in the Bible. High on that list is his leadership style. Aaron had good leadership qualities but on the other hand, he was also plagued with negative leadership traits. Aaron was one of the church leaders in the wilderness besides Moses, Joshua, and Miriam. Aaron was the elder brother of Moses. He was three years older than Moses, according to Exodus 7:7. Because of his oratorial capabilities, God appointed him to be the spokesperson for Moses who was a *stammerer*, Exodus 4:14. Together with his sister Miriam, they were the leaders assisting Moses to lead the children of Israel to the Promised Land. He later became the high priest after God instituted the Tabernacle.

One of the positive leadership qualities of Aaron is that he was *obedient*. Being the eldest brother of Moses, it was culturally expected that he would give orders to Moses and not get orders from Moses. God's strategy was to give Moses instructions and Aaron would implement them for miracles to happen in Egypt. This needed an obedient leader and Aaron was that man. The result was that great miracles happened in Egypt that eventually brought the deliverance of the Israelites from the bondage of Pharoah and the Egyptians.

Leadership of Aaron was plagued with negative leadership traits, as well. Aaron was a men-pleaser, compromiser, and indecisive in his leadership, characteristics that had catastrophic results for himself and the Israelites. In Exodus 32:23, we have a record of a catastrophic event that happened in Israel where three thousand people died in one day. Looking at the story, one thing is evident, these people died because of the *men pleaser*, and compromising leadership style of Aaron. God had called Moses and Joshua to the mountain to receive the Ten Commandments. This mission took forty days to complete.

Back in the camp, the children of Israel had gotten impatient with the delay of Moses. For some reason, they convinced Aaron to build them a golden calf idol to be their god. One wonders how they were able to convince Aaron to stoop that low. But on the bottom side, Aaron did all that because he wanted to please these people instead of pleasing God. A leader should aspire to please God at all times, rather than people. The apostle Paul teaches in his epistle to the Galatians that when we seek to please men instead of God, we cannot qualify to be servants of God.

"For do I now persuade men, or God? Or do I seek to please men? For if I still pleased men, I would not be a bondservant of Christ" Galatians 1:10, NKJV.

As men, sometimes we find ourselves in such situations where we compromise our leadership when we seek to please people, rather than God. This is not easy when it comes to leading our homes, especially when your spouse asks you to make a decision that is not pleasing to God. It leaves you with a lot of condemnation in your heart. The response that Aaron gave Moses when asked about the golden calf situation shows one of the weaknesses that man has had since the time of Adam and Eve.

Instead of Aaron admitting the mistake, he throws the blame on the children of Israel as having forced him to mold the idol. A leader should be able to take the blame when in a mistake to avoid making the same blunder next time. When Adam and Eve sinned against God, the same script played to their detriment. Adam blamed Eve for the disobedience. Eve, on the other hand, blamed the serpent for her sin. None of them were ready to accept the blame.

Repentance only happens when we acknowledge our mistakes before God. Naturally, man will tend to cover his faults, which leads to a lack of progress in our lives. The scriptures teach us that prosperity is a product of the confession of sin.

"He who covers his sins will not prosper, But whoever confesses and forsakes them will have mercy" Proverbs 28:13, NKJV.

A good leader should be willing to accept blame when in error. This *blame game* plays out a lot in marriage relationships. Marital problems occur more when both spouses are overprotective and do not admit mistakes when in the wrong. In another incident, Miriam, the sister of Moses, became leprous because together with Aaron, she was involved in gossiping about Moses. The fact that Aaron never rebuked Miriam when they talked negatively about Moses leaves much room for speculation. It is possible that Aaron feared offending Miriam, hence the failure to correct, or stop, her from talking ill about Moses.

Gossip can destroy God's work. This is an area that affects us leaders so much. Looking at my own life and ministry, I see several instances where the work of God was affected because I feared to rebuke the members when they were doing wrong.

There was a time when our church went through a split because some of the leaders were discontent with certain aspects of the ministry. This was all started by one of our leaders who gathered other members to complain about issues. Though I knew that this was going on, I did not confront the brethren concerned. The main reason for this was primarily because I did not want to injure their feelings, plus the fact that I also took it lightly. Eventually, these brethren caused a split that resulted in over one hundred members being misled and they formed another fellowship in the area. Though some of the brethren later on came to know the truth and came back to our church, some were misled and lost spiritual and moral direction.

This is the type of mistake that Aaron's type of leadership creates, as well as ours, if we fail to walk, and lead, according to God's Word. As men, we are called to provide leadership, especially in our homes. Wisdom therefore entails that we build our capacity towards positive virtues of leadership, rather than the negative ones. This will result in strong families and gospel ministries.

Hezekiah

Fred H. McCree

"Now it came to pass in the third year of Hoshea the son of Elah, king of
Israel, that Hezekiah the son of Ahaz, king of Judah, began to reign."
Joshua 1:1-3

We live in a day an age where some men feel as if prayer is not important. It's funny because we seek advice from our friends and family before seeking God for the answer. As a man, praying to God is necessary. Prayer is our communication method to keep God first in every area of our lives. In Luke 18:1, Jesus made it plain to pray continuously. When I need advice, I pray. If I need help, I pray. When I need peace, I pray. If my money is funny, I pray. If I am having relationship and martial issues, I pray. And if I am sick, I pray. Prayer is not about getting things from God, but it is about developing an intimate relationship with God. Moreover, The Lord knows what we stand in need of, and He desires a personal relationship with us, as well.

Furthermore, when I think about the Bible, there are so many prayer warriors mentioned. Their prayers did not bounce off the ceiling, but actually got God to move on their behalf. Jesus was a *prayer warrior*. Moses was a *prayer warrior*. David was a *prayer warrior*, and Joshua was a *prayer warrior*. However, there is another *prayer warrior* that I would like to draw your attention to. His name is Hezekiah. In 2 King 20:1-11, states:

"In those days Hezekiah became terminally ill. The prophet Isaiah son of Amoz came and said to him, "This is what the LORD says: "Set your house in order, for you are about to die; you will not recover. Then Hezekiah turned his face to the wall and prayed to the LORD, "Please, LORD, remember how I have walked before you faithfully and whole-heartedly and have done what pleases you." And Hezekiah wept bitterly. Isaiah had not yet gone out of the inner courtyard when the word of the LORD came to him: "Go back and tell Hezekiah, the leader of my people, 'This is what the LORD God of your ancestor David says: I have heard your prayer; I have seen your tears. Look, I will heal you. On the third day from now you will go up to the LORD's temple. I will add fifteen years to your life. I will rescue you and this city from the grasp of the king of Assyria. I will defend this city for my sake and for the sake of my servant David.' Then Isaiah said, "Bring a lump of pressed figs." So, they brought it and applied it to his infected skin, and he recovered. Hezekiah had asked Isaiah, "What is the sign that the LORD will heal me and that I will go up to the LORD's temple on the third day?" Isaiah said, "This is the sign to you from the LORD that he will do what he has promised: Should the shadow go ahead ten steps or go back ten steps?" Then Hezekiah answered, "It is easy for the shadow to lengthen ten steps. No, let the shadow go back ten steps." So the prophet Isaiah called out to the LORD, and he brought the shadow back the ten steps it had descended on the stairway of Ahaz."

In the section before this text, we find King Hezekiah who has done everything right to please God. He got the whole kingdom in order from worshipping idols. Now, we come to this text in 1 King 20:1-11, we find King Hezekiah sick with some kind of illness. The prophet Isaiah came to him and told him to get his house in order, because he was about to die. Instead of Hezekiah calling his friends, or searching for the answer from fortune tellers, he prayed and cried out to God. As a result, before the man of God Isaiah could leave the courtyard, God heard King Hezekiah and added fifteen more years to his life. The text said, *in three days he would be healed.* So, what is the point? A lot of us are just like King Hezekiah. We get shocking news all the time; sometimes, that shocking news brings death to our spirit. But regardless of what we face, we can rest and be assured that when we pray, God hears us and will answer our prayer. It's interesting when I look back over my life. I can relate to King Hezekiah. I lived my life to please God.

Seven years ago, I was in the military. I weighed 300.6 pounds. The military could not figure out what was wrong with me. I told my co-worker, "I do not know what is wrong with me, but my God will fix it." I prayed and cried out to God to heal me. I knew my condition was shortening my life. I had high blood pressure, diabetes, and everything else you can think of. I kept praying and then one day, I went to work and the doctor sent me to an endocrinologist. The endocrinologist diagnosed me with "Cushing's Disease."

This *Cushing's Disease* is caused by a tumor in your brain pressing on your pituitary gland. The specialist found the causes and I went to Stanford Medical Hospital to have it surgically removed. I dealt with this thing for seven years but now, the tumor is removed. As a result, there is no more high blood pressure or diabetes, nor anything else you can think of. Now, I weigh under 190 pounds. God heard my prayer. Thank God for answering our prayers.

God healed me just like He healed King Hezekiah because I prayed. I am here to tell somebody, trust God! He can heal whatever your situation is. He can add life back to your situation. Since He did it for me and King Hezekiah, I know He will do it for you. One of the things I appreciate God for is that He is not a respecter of persons, but He respects principles found in His Word.

There is healing power when we seek God in prayer. God worked on King Hezekiah's and my behalf. He will do the same for you! God can answer your prayers, if you believe, and seek Him first with faith in prayer. I do not know who I am talking to, just remember; no matter what you are going through, prayer can change it. Let me pray for you now!

Father God, the Creator of the Universe, the Alpha and Omega, the Beginning and the End, and the Savior of our souls. We confess our sins to You now. God, we ask if there is anything in us that is not like You Lord, please forgive us. Help us in the areas of our lives that we fall short. God, I pray for the individual reading this devotion. I pray to You Lord that whatever they are dealing with, or going through, I pray You would heal their situation. If it is sickness, heal it. If it is a relationship situation, fix it. If it is a money situation, supply it. If they stand in need, Lord, do it. I pray whatever their situation is God, move on their behalf.

God, I know You are able to do abundantly, exceedingly above and beyond what we can think or imagine. Lord, I speak healing over them right now. Lord, we expect You to move, and we have faith that You will. We seal this prayer with our faith. Thank You Lord for hearing our prayer, in Jesus' name, Amen!

Daniel

Daniel Edman

"But Daniel made up his mind that he would not defile himself with the king's choice food or with the wine which he drank; so he sought permission from the commander of the officials that he might not defile himself."
Daniel 1:8

D aniel's life is an example of how we can live a life of integrity in a culture that is trying to form us into its mold. Integrity is something that has always been very important to me. Integrity means *to be honest*. It means to have *strong moral principles*.

To me, in my own words, it means doing the right thing even when no one else is looking. Daniel always made sure he was doing the right thing, according to God, whether he was rewarded for it or thrown into a den of lions. This is how I choose to live my life, as well. I didn't always live this way.

I grew up in a house that never went to church. We didn't make things of God important. My family was very dysfunctional. This led me to be rebellious, to live my life the way I wanted. I didn't want anything to do with God, until I was a teenager. I actually went to church because of a girl; I went to church until I graduated high school. Even in all this time I was going to church, my life was unchanged by it. After high school, I walked away altogether.

This was my life until finally one day, in my early twenties, my brother invited me to a business conference. I didn't know it at the time but the founders of this business were Christians. I heard a common theme at this conference. People kept telling me if I wanted to see why they were so successful, I was to come back Sunday morning. I was intrigued enough to go back on Sunday. That Sunday changed my life. I found out that their success was because of their faith in God. In this service, they had an altar call; they said, "If you want to ask God into your heart, come up" and I decided to go up. I felt like the enemy was trying to hold me back but it just made me more determined to get up there.

Once I got up there, I asked God into my heart and everything changed. I wouldn't say there was immediate change. But gradually over the years, God has changed the way I think, the way I act, and the way I respond to Him. I went from a man who had no integrity, not wanting to be a man of God, to a man who values integrity and values God in my life.

Just like Daniel, I have learned not to compromise my standards. The world will do everything in its power to get you to compromise on God's Word. I will do everything in my power to not let that happen. All I do has to line up with God's Word and His will for me. I try not to let the world influence me. I look to God's Word and ways and try my best to not stray from that. I am still human and make mistakes. But I know Holy Spirit will help me up every time I fall down.

One lesson I learned from Daniel is that he was unwilling to compromise his standards. He determined, or made up his mind, that he would follow God's ways no matter what. He didn't care who came against him or how they threatened him to bow to what they wanted. He focused only on God!

As a semi driver, I am exposed to many types of people and many ways of the world. When I am driving down the interstate or back roads, I have people pass me and give me rude gestures; they'll slow down on purpose to play games. I could lower myself to their level and do the same thing to them. What I choose to do instead is honor God! I made up my mind to not defile myself by reacting in a way that would not give honor to the One I follow. Another example that comes to mind is from a friend of mine. He needed help fixing his car. I went to his house and while I was there, he showed me a picture on his phone. It was of a half-naked woman. As soon as I saw the picture, I turned my head away and said, "Please don't show me stuff like that again." I told him that because I have made up my mind not to defile my mind or my marriage. The only woman God wants me to look at is my wife.

When I was younger, I had an addiction to pornography. If I allow those temptations into my life in any way, that could lure me back to my old self. But God delivered me from that and I refuse to dishonor God, or my wife, by letting those temptations enter my life. I will keep my focus on my God alone!

One last example that comes to mind has to do with someone who is close to me. Within the last year, this person and I have been talking more about our spiritual life and walk and what we believe. Anytime that his beliefs did not line up with the Word of God, Holy Spirit would share with me what verse could be used to combat that lie. For example, he believes that he can enter Heaven through a state of mind. He believes everyone can get to Heaven the same way.. After listening to him, Holy Spirit brought John 14:6 to mind. Which says,

"Jesus said to him, "I am the way, the truth and the life. No one comes to the Father except through Me" NKJV.

There is a Heaven and the only way we get there is through Jesus! There is no other way. Another belief we talked about is believing in the written Word. He believes that we cannot trust the Bible because it was written by man. Holy Spirit brought 2 Peter 1:21 to mind. Which says,

"For prophecy never came by the will of man, but holy men of God spoke as they were moved by the Holy Spirit" NKJV.

Another scripture He brought to me was 2 Timothy 3:16.

"All Scripture is given by inspiration of God, and is profitable for doctrine, for reproof, for correction, for instruction in righteousness" NKJV.

I share this with you to show you that people will try to defile your mind with lies and beliefs that are of the world. The solution is to turn to God and His Word to see what He says, and go in that way.

Another lesson I learned is the importance of *commitment*. Daniel was committed to doing right in God's eyes so much that he was willing to die for it. Let me explain. In Daniel 6, Darius the Mede thought a lot of Daniel and gave him a high position. There were some men who were jealous of Daniel. This jealousy drove them to trick Darius into issuing a decree. Daniel 6:7 says,

"All the commissioners of the kingdom, the prefects and the satraps, the high officials and the governors have consulted together that the king should establish a statute and enforce an injunction that anyone who makes a petition to any god or man besides you, O king, for thirty days, shall be cast into the lions' den" NASB.

Daniel knew about the decree. He knew and it did not deter him. The Bible says that *"he continued kneeling on his knees three times a day, praying and giving thanks before his God, as he had been doing previously"* Daniel 6:10. He did not try to hide his devotion to God. Because of this, the jealous men went before the king and told him about Daniel and the king had to keep his word. He threw Daniel into the lion's den. He was in there all night. The Bible says the king went in haste to the lion's den. The king cries out, *"Daniel, servant of the living God, has your God, whom you constantly serve, been able to deliver you from the lions?"* Daniel 6:20, NASB. Notice the king said, "servant of the living God." Daniel's decision didn't just impact him, it also impacted the king. The king saw all that Daniel was willing to go through for God and must have thought there must be something to Daniel's God. Either way, after this incident, the king knew God was real! The Bible says,

"Then Darius the king wrote to all the peoples, nations and men of every language who were living in all the land: "May your peace

abound! I make a decree that in all the dominion of my kingdom men are to fear and tremble before the God of Daniel; For He is the living God and enduring forever, And His kingdom is one which will not be destroyed, And His dominion will be forever. He delivers and rescues and performs signs and wonders in heaven and on earth, Who has also delivered Daniel from the power of the lions" Daniel 6:25-27, NASB.

Through this story, we see that our commitment can and will affect others. It will affect them in a negative way or positive. Some people will not understand why we stay committed to God but others, like King Darius, will see our commitment and will know there is a God. That's what our life needs to do, bring glory to God in such a way that it will draw others to Him!

Daniel is an inspiration to me to have the courage to stay committed to God no matter what others do to me, no matter what the consequences may be. It will all be worth it in the end!

Samson

Tim Sittig

"So the woman bore a son and called his name Samson; and the child grew, and the Lord blessed him." Judges 13:24

Foolish ways hinder God's work and plans for our lives. This was the case in my life. I was raised by Godly parents. Devotions and before bedtime prayers were a daily part of life. As far as childhood's go, mine seemed to be revolving around God from an early age. At the age of sixteen, at a winter youth retreat, I got saved. Up until this point, I knew quite a few Bible verses, but didn't really put it all together. Here, a youth leader showed me how I was separated from God by sin. It was a scary thing to realize. The news that Jesus died on the Cross to make a way back to Him was a relief, indeed.

Samson was set apart by God before he was even conceived in his mother's womb. The angel of the Lord came to his mother and said, *"And the Angel of the Lord appeared to the woman and said to her, "Indeed now, you are barren and have borne no children, but you shall conceive and bear a son"* Judges 13:3

Just like me, Samson was raised to know the Lord. He was reared by his mother and his father, Manoah, per the instructions of the Angel of the Lord. He was not to drink wine or any other fermented drink, and was forbidden to eat anything unclean. He was also not to put a razor to his head; he was not to cut his hair, because he was considered a Nazarite to God from the womb. My life was surely not as strict or stringent as Samson's, but being raised by Godly parents, my parents surely had planned for me to serve God and to walk in His ways.

Forward about four years, and I had moved out with a couple of guys from my neighborhood, and we got our first apartment. The freedom to do what we wanted, when we wanted, proved to be my downfall. Quickly and foolishly, I might add, I began to fall away from what I knew. I began to live so much like the unsaved friends of mine that I was just like them. I, like Samson, seemed to do as I pleased and left God out most of the time.

"Now Samson went down to Timnah, and saw a woman in Timnah of the daughters of the Philistines. So he went up and told his father and mother, saying, "I have seen a woman in Timnah of the daughters of the Philistines; now therefore, get her for me as a wife." Then his father and mother said to him, "Is there no woman among the daughters of your brethren, or among all my people, that you must go and get a wife from the uncircumcised Philistines?" And Samson said to his father, "Get her for me, for she pleases me well." But his father and mother did not know that it was of the Lord—that He was seeking an occasion to move against the Philistines. For at that time the Philistines had dominion over Israel. So Samson went down to Timnah with his father and mother, and came to the vineyards of Timnah. Now to his surprise, a young lion came roaring against him. And the Spirit of the Lord came mightily upon him, and he tore the lion apart as one would have torn apart a young goat, though he had nothing in his hand. But he did not tell his father or his mother what he had done. Then he went down and talked with the woman; and she pleased Samson well. After some time, when he returned to get her, he turned aside to see the carcass of the lion. And behold, a swarm of bees and honey were in the carcass of the lion. He took some of it in his hands and went along, eating. When he came to his father and mother, he gave some to them, and they also ate. But he did not tell them that he had taken the honey out of the carcass of the lion."
Judges 14:1-9

Samson clearly displayed a sense of pride, arrogance, and entitlement in his request to his father and mother to "go get her for me". His father inquired of him why he could not find a wife from among his brethren, or his people. This was a father trying to guard his son from possible dangerous consequences. Samson would not hear. He went and did *as he pleased*. In doing so, it says they "came to the *vineyards* of Timnah". The Angel of the Lord clearly warned Samson's father and mother that he was not to *drink of the vine*, nor any fermented drink. The Bible warns us to:

"Drink water from your own cistern, And running water from your own well" Proverbs 5:15

This was not only a natural warning, but also a spiritual cautioning. Samson was entering into spiritual temptation with every refusal to not only obey his parents, but also the commandment of God concerning his Nazarite vows. It goes on to say, "Then he went down and talked with the woman; and she *pleased* Samson well. After some time, when he returned to get her, he turned aside to see the carcass of the lion. And behold, a swarm of bees and honey were in the carcass of the lion. **He took some of it in his hands and went along, eating.**"

Samson had now broken two of his Nazarite vows in one trip! He had now touched, and eaten, that which was unclean in God's eyes. And to make matters worse, he had also given it to his parents to eat; not telling them it had come from the dead carcass of a lion that he had torn to pieces with his bare hands. We must understand that our disobedience, our sin, not only affects our spiritual walk, but it also affects those connected to us. Sin, when it reaches its full capacity, brings death to everything and everyone around us.

"Then, when desire has conceived, it gives birth to sin; and sin, when it is full-grown, brings forth death" James 1:15.

Samson's lustful desires had given birth to sin in his life. Looking back, I am so thankful that the Lord did not leave me to my own desires, but led me back to Him. I do, however, think about from time to time what would have been possible had I not so foolishly dabbled in the world for so long. It seems like a real waste of time but I guess God's mercy and grace could only really be understood by me through my falling so short. Thank God that He is so loving and patient when His own go astray. God still had a plan for Samson's life though he betrayed his vows at every turn. Samson's strength to rip apart a lion was testament of the anointing on his life, but due to his arrogance, he was digging himself deeper and deeper into sin.

"And they said to him, "Pose your riddle, that we may hear it." So he said to them: "Out of the eater came something to eat, And out of the strong came something sweet." Now for three days they could not explain the riddle" Judges 13b-14.

Samson was now mocking God's commandment over his life to abstain from such profane things. He was outwardly boasting of his disobedience, not thinking God was taking note of it all. The men told Samson's wife that if she could not get him to reveal to her what the riddle meant, that they would burn her and her father's house. She eventually enticed Samson to tell her the truth and she gave the men the answer. Samson was livid that she betrayed him and that these men used her to do so; therefore, he went and killed thirty of their men. Soon after he returned from his father's house, he went to get his wife, but she had been given to his best man, a companion. Samson became very angry and took three-hundred foxes and tied them tail to tail and lit them with a torch and burned up their grain fields, vineyards, and olive groves. The Philistines retaliated by burning up the woman and her father's house entirely.

Once again, our sin not only affects us, but everything and everyone connected to us. Samson retaliated back by slaughtering many of the Philistines. He then ran and retreated to the cleft of the rock in Etam. The Philistines then came up to Judah looking for him and the men of Judah went to get Samson to turn him over to the Philistines. They tied him up with ropes and as the Philistines came up against him, the Spirit of the Lord came upon Samson and the ropes burned like fire and broke off his hands.

"He found a fresh jawbone of a donkey, reached out his hand and took it, and killed a thousand men with it. Then Samson said: "With the jawbone of a donkey, Heaps upon heaps, With the jawbone of a donkey I have slain a thousand men!" Judges 15:15-16

Again, the Philistines were ruling over Israel at this time. God had a plan and Samson was the one He anointed to carry it out. God has a plan for each of our lives. He has an assignment that only we can carry out for His ultimate glory. We may try to run from it, or we may fall into great sin and temptation along the way that may hinder us from reaching our full potential in Christ, but God never gives up on us. The Bible says, *"He will never leave us nor forsake us."* God continued to super-naturally grant Samson the strength to defeat the Philistines, His ene-mies, at every turn. I am encouraged that no matter how far I may have strayed from God, at that time in my life, He was still right there waiting for me to return to Him. He was waiting from Samson, as well.

In his final test, Samson ran into Delilah… the greatest deception he would face in his life. One meaning of the name Delilah is "one who weakens". The Bible states that he "loved" Delilah.

"Afterward it happened that he loved a woman in the Valley of Sorek, whose name was Delilah. And the lords of the Philistines came up to her and said to her, "Entice him, and find out where his great strength lies, and by what means we may overpower him, that we may bind him to afflict him; and every one of us will give you eleven hundred pieces of silver" Judges 16:4-5

Delilah did just as his first wife and drilled him until he finally told her all that was in his heart, the truth of who he was and the source of his strength, the anointing upon his life. She revealed that his hair, his seven locks, were the foundation of his strength and if his head were shaved, he would become weak like other men. After she lulled him to sleep and the man came to shave his head, Delilah shouted one last time, "The Philistines are upon you, Samson!"

"So he awoke from his sleep, and said, "I will go out as before, at other times, and shake myself free!" But he did not know that **the Lord had departed from him***"* Judges 16:20

Samson's time was up! He had betrayed the entirety of His Nazarite vow to the Lord and God removed His anointing from his life. I don't know about you, but this is a very scary place to find yourself. God gives us more chances in this life than we deserve yet many of us continue to disobey His voice and reject His Word. We think we have all the time in the world to get it together and that we can come back to Him when we get ready. Samson thought he could simply "shake himself free" as he did many times before, but this time was different.

"Then the Philistines took him and put out his eyes, and brought him down to Gaza. They bound him with bronze fetters, and he became a grinder in the prison" Judges 16:21

They stook his eyesight, his vision… the only thing left, so they thought, that would hinder him from getting free.

"However, the hair of his head **began to grow again** *after it had been shaven"* Judges 16:22

Remember, the work God begins within us, He will complete, Philippians 1:6. Though Samson was blinded physically, God was doing something within him spiritually. God allowed Samson's natural eyesight to be taken, so that he could finally SEE what He called and anointed him to do for Him.

"Then Samson called to the Lord, saying, "O Lord God, remember me, I pray! Strengthen me, I pray, just this once, O God, that I may with one blow take vengeance on the Philistines for my two eyes!" And Samson took hold of the two middle pillars which supported the temple, and he braced himself against them, one on his right and the other on his left. Then Samson said, "Let me die with the Philistines!" And he pushed with all his might, and the temple fell on the lords and all the people who were in it. So the dead that he killed at his death were more than he had killed in his life" Judges 16:28-30

SAMSON

May we take heed to the lessons learned through the life of Samson. Obedience is always better than sacrifice. God desires to protect us from temptation and sin. He puts these safeguards in place not to harm us, but to help us. His plans for us are good, and He knows and sees so far ahead of us. My we learn to trust Him and let Him use our lives for His glory!

A Man After God's Own Heart

Graham Pitts

"But now thy kingdom shall not continue: the Lord hath sought him a man after his own heart, and the Lord hath commanded him to be captain over his people, because thou hast not kept that which the Lord commanded thee." 1 Samuel 13:14

B *ut God is the Judge: He puts down one and exalts another"* Psalm 75:7, NKJV.

"So it was, when they came, that he looked at Eliab and said, "Surely the Lord's anointed is before Him!" But the Lord said to Samuel, "Do not look at his appearance or at his physical stature, because I have refused him. For the Lord does not see as man sees; for man looks at the outward appearance, but the Lord looks at the heart." I Samuel 16:6-7, NKJV.

God knew who He had picked for the role but let the prophet Samuel use his earthly logic and wisdom to pick the eldest brother Eliab, and quite rightly so, because of tradition and the social normalities of the day. I have found in my own walk to be just as guilty as Samuel, it's far too easy to look at the earthly qualities in a person and question if it's God's will for them to be used in that capacity, because we do not see as the Lord sees. So, I have also received much resistance to God's decisions over my own life, because a man reaps what he sows and so it is for me.

"And Samuel said to Jesse, "Are all the young men here?" Then he said, "There remains yet the youngest, and there he is, keeping the sheep." And Samuel said to Jesse, "Send and bring him. For we will not sit down till he comes here." So he sent and brought him in. Now he was ruddy, with bright eyes, and good-looking. And the Lord said, "Arise, anoint him; for this is the one!" Then Samuel took the horn of oil and anointed him in the midst of his brothers; and the Spirit of the Lord came upon David from that day forward. So Samuel arose and went to Ramah" I Samuel 16:11-13, NKJV.

David, at this time, was in the fields tending to his father's business, not to be brought in with his brothers, the sons of Jesse, due to his age and role in the family. I also found myself in a similar position, working in the world away from any of my brothers in Christ and tending the flock allotted to me in life, when the Lord sent for me through another. Many have questioned the length of my walk with the Lord and quite rightly so, there are by far many others more qualified, dignified, and deserving to be chosen for what the Lord has graciously set before me. I found it hard, and I still do, to accept a calling from the Lord, when I'm just a normal carpenter, with a normal background who had completely walked away from God for many years and only returned to God a few months prior.

I had so much disbelief and self-doubt in what had been spoken over me, so much so, I had asked for confirmation from the Lord before I would consider what had been said. The Lord honoured my prayer and gave me a strange dream that made no sense to me at the time, but I knew *Who* had given it to me and that very same week, I was at a prophetic evening at my church when the dream came back to me. I laughed out loud during the meeting thinking to myself, *if anyone can interpret a dream, surely a prophet can.* So, at the end of the meeting, I spoke through an interpreter to the visiting Brazilian prophet about the strange dream I had, to which the prophet started confirming everything I had asked prior to the Lord. So, how much harder would it had been for David to accept his calling?

Sons Of Purpose

"The Lord is my light and my salvation; Whom shall, I fear? The Lord is the strength of my life; Of whom shall I be afraid" Psalm 27:1, NKJV.

"David said to Saul, "Let no one lose heart on account of this Philistine; your servant will go and fight him." "You are not able to go against this Philistine to fight with him, for you are a youth, and he a man of war from his youth" 1 Samuel 17:32-33, NKJV.

We see Saul doubtful at this young David when he uses his earthly eyes and wisdom and I can relate to the profoundness of the situation. David was ordained by the Lord for a task and a purpose; he also had the heart of a warrior, and the anointing was on him. David stepped out with confidence in the Lord, not in Saul's ill-fitting armor from a man that would serve to hinder his calling. But in the confidence of a faithful servant to the Lord. I have stepped out like David and each time the Lord has blessed the outcomes because they are in line with His calling and each time, prayer has been the backbone of the action. The Lord equips us with His full spiritual armor to tackle our adversary, to be able to overcome him. I have had multiple Saul's in my own walk who have been doubtful and dismissive, and I have no doubts that you have as well, but when the Lord has called you by name to be a *Son of Purpose*, you must stand and be counted.

"Moreover David said, "The Lord, who delivered me from the paw of the lion and from the paw of the bear, He will deliver me from the hand of this Philistine." And Saul said to David, "Go, and the Lord be with you!" 1 Samuel 17:37, NKJV.

David had gone through trial and tribulation in the wilderness; God had allowed the beasts of the Earth to come against him for his future preparation, but what does David say about this? *"The Lord, who delivered me from..."* So I, too, can recognize the battles I have faced in my wilderness. God has allowed the beasts of the Earth to come against me in my own life and I have wrestled with them for many years, in the form of strongholds, addictions, and self-hate spanning decades. But when I have come into full submission to God, only then has the Lord delivered me from them.

"Then David put his hand in his bag and took out a stone; and he slung it and struck the Philistine in his forehead, so that the stone sank into his forehead, and he fell on his face to the earth. So David prevailed over the Philistine with a sling and a stone and struck the Philistine and killed him. But there was no sword in the hand of David" 1 Samuel 17:49, NKJV.

Not all our *Goliaths* are standing towering over us in bronze armor, but our enemy is most certainly here to stand in our way and to try to defy our purpose. I have found it could be a comment to strip a prophetic word from us like a taunt from the giant Goliath himself, or his mighty shield to block our callings through obstruction and hinderance. But if God has prepared the man, He has also prepared the way. He will always lead you to where He needs you to be, do not be afraid. God's words are the smooth stones and when we read His Word and meditate on it, we fill our own *Shepard's bag*. And, in our trials and tribulations, no matter the situation, the double-edged sword of God's Word will be brought forward with the guidance of the Holy Spirit and used mightily for breakthrough and victory in Him.

Repentance Brings Restoration
"The steps of a good man are ordered by the Lord, And He delights in his way. Though he fall, he shall not be utterly cast down; For the Lord upholds him with His hand" Psalm 37:23-24, NKJV.

"So David's anger was greatly aroused against the man, and he said to Nathan, "As the Lord lives, the man who has done this shall surely die!" 2 Samuel 12:5, NKJV.

Here is a man with a heart after the Lord but still *a man* and we have seen another side of him. David had sent a loyal soldier to his death because he himself had committed adultery with the soldier's wife and conceived a child with her. We have seen the positive sides to David in his youth; he wrote many a Psalm in awe and love to God but as a man, he had his own flaws and failures, as we all do. David, upon hearing the parable about the sheep from Nathan, became angry and wrathful without knowing it was about himself. I have heard things myself and jumped straight into the judge's seat with the conclusion of *guilty*. I have walked away from God completely because of doubts and thoughts, and walked away from the gift of life God had given me and, in all rights, deserve death just as David did.

"So David said to Nathan, "I have sinned against the Lord." And Nathan said to David, "The Lord also has put away your sin; you shall not die. However, because by this deed you have given great occasion to the enemies of the Lord to blaspheme, the child also who is born to you shall surely die" 2 Samuel 12:13-14, NKJV.

There is grace and redemption when we cry out to God for our sins in true repentance just like the parable of the prodigal son. David finally comes to his senses and fully repents upon the conviction in his heart. He is swiftly corrected and disciplined for this sin. I had to walk through the wilderness of life for over ten years after walking away from God, making bad decision after bad decision to the point of complete self-hatred and the plans in place to end my life. But I cried out to God with true repentance in a last-ditch effort, asking for Jesus Christ to take the hate and anger out of my heart. As I was crying His name out, the bedroom door slammed closed and from that day forward, God opened new doors in my life. I don't know how different my life would have been had I not walked away from God and made bad decisions; however, I know my God turns our bad situations into His goodness. I received deliverance from my strongholds, addictions, mindsets, and emotions, and I am now in training to be able to pay it forward. God doesn't need Goliaths, he needs *David's*, men after His own heart.

I pray for anyone reading this message, if you are struggling like I was, reach out to God and to mature Christians because there is no burden God cannot take off your shoulders. He loves each and every one of us no matter what we have said or what we have done. When we turn to Him and ask for forgiveness, He will show love and compassion and greet us with open arms and forgiveness.

"As for God, His way is perfect; The word of the Lord is proven; He is a shield to all who trust in Him" Psalm 18:30, NKJV.

A Psalm To The Lord—Graham Pitts

Finger picking strings (1 is low E, 6 is High E)
G—1456 D—3456 Em—2456
C—2456

Intro: G D Em C

V1
```
G                    D
```
I, I come to Your voice
```
        Em
```
I come to bow down
```
            C
```
In Your Presence
```
G                         D
```
Oh my Lord, Oh my King
```
    Em           C
```
Jesus Christ, Lord of my heart
```
    G
```
Lord of all

V2
```
  G           D
```
Shepherd, over my life
```
        Em
```
May this tongue
```
        C
```
Sing Your praise
```
            G
```
```
D
```
Joined by the angels, by Your
side
```
        Em            C
```
May this praise, be like honey
```
        G
```

V3
```
G                    D
```
Lord, You tell the sun to shine
```
        Em
```
On my face
```
                    C
```
To warm my days
```
        G                    D
```
Oh my Lord, You hold the stars
```
                    Em
```
```
C
```
In their place, they twinkle at
Your voice
```
            G
```
At Your voice

V4
```
G                         D
```
The, the seasons they eagerly
await
```
            Em        C
```
For Your sake, for You Lord
```
                G
```
So may my life's work
```
                D
```
Be like a summer's day
```
            Em        C
```
To You Lord, Lord of all
```
            G
```
Lord of all

Job

Edwin Rideout

"There was a man in the land of Uz whose name was Job, and that man was blameless and upright, one who feared God and turned away from evil."
Job 1:1

Job started almost every day by *sipping on a freshly brewed coffee* while immersing his soul in the stunning spectacle of the nearby mountain range. His family was healthy, business was booming, and life was good. However, that morning, lurking near the surface, was an uneasiness. His adult children were holding another party—he worried what could ensue. Returning to "refill his coffee," he noticed one of his servants rushing toward him; panting for his breath, he blurted out:

"The oxen were plowing and the donkeys grazing in the field next to us when Sabeans attacked. They stole the animals and killed the field hands. I'm the only one to get out alive and tell you what happened. "While he was still talking, another messenger arrived and said, "Bolts of lightning struck the sheep and the shepherds and fried them—burned them to a crisp. I'm the only one to get out alive and tell you what happened." While he was still talking, another messenger arrived and said, "Chaldeans coming from three directions raided the camels and massacred the camel drivers. I'm the only one to get out alive and tell you what happened. "While he was still talking, another messenger arrived and said, "Your children were having a party...a tornado swept

in off the desert and struck the house. It collapsed on them, and they died. I'm the only one to get out alive and tell you what happened" Job 1:14-19, MES.

Such a tale borders on bizarre. Ten adult children, along with numerous employees, were tragically killed, and his business was obliterated. Who could bear the news of such incredible loss in a brief period? If this is not enough, a few verses further along, we discover,

"Satan went out from the presence of the Lord and struck Job with loathsome sores from the sole of his foot to the crown of his head. And he took a piece of broken pottery with which to scrape himself while he sat in the ashes. Then his wife said to him, "Do you still hold fast your integrity? Curse God and die." But he said to her, "You speak as one of the foolish women would speak. Shall we receive good from God, and shall we not receive evil?" Job 2:7-10a, ESV.

And, to add insult to injury, his best friends visited him. They sat with him in silence for seven days, after which they each took turns accusing him of injustice, pride, and violating God's holy standards. During his darkest hours, the Bible says, *"In all this Job did not sin with his lips"* Job 10b, ESV. Instead, he affirmed his confidence in God. Here are just a few of his astounding statements:

- Job 33:4—The Spirit of God has made me, and the breath of the Almighty gives me life.
- Job 10:11-12—You clothed me with skin and flesh and knit me together with bones and sinews. You have granted me life and steadfast love, and Your care has preserved my spirit.
- Job 13:15a—Though he slays me, I will hope in him.
- Job 19:26—And after my skin has been destroyed, in my flesh, I shall see God.
- Job 27:3-4—As long as my breath is in me, and the spirit of God is in my nostrils, my lips will not speak falsehood, and my tongue will not utter deceit.

The story of Job stands as a powerful tribute to resilience—the ability to endure and bounce back from adversity—and to integrity, marked by honesty and unwavering ethical values. Despite losing his wealth, children, and health, Job maintains his integrity by refusing to curse God or abandon his faith. His resilience is demonstrated through his endurance and persistence in seeking understanding and justice from God, even during his profound suffering.

I have a friend who experienced tremendous losses. His youngest daughter died from Neuroblastoma at the tender age of twenty-eight months. A few years later, he and his wife stood by the side of their eldest daughter and son-in-law as they cuddled their precious stillborn daughter. Two years later, his wife went to be with Jesus following a yearlong battle with cancer. And if that is not enough for any man to endure, four years afterward, he held his precious grandson in his arms while standing beside the coffins of his daughter, his son-in-law, and grandson—brother to the one he carried in his arms—all victims of a tragic motor vehicle accident. Today, Ron is an encourager; he possesses incredible faith in God. He has devoted his life to raising his grandson and serving God and others. This is possible because of the resolutions Ron made during the darkest nights of his soul. He chose to live. He pursued joy. He leaned into God. He elected to love.

Ron's journey through grief and loss mirrors Job's resilience and integrity. Like Job, Ron faced unimaginable tragedies yet chose to continue living a life anchored in faith and purpose. His decision to raise his grandson, serve others, and remain faithful to God amidst his losses showcases a similar steadfastness and moral fortitude. Ron's life exemplifies how resilience and integrity can guide one through the darkest times, transforming personal pain into a source of strength and encouragement for others.

C. S. Lewis said, "Every time you make a choice, you are turning your soul, the part that chooses, into something a little different than it was before. Taking your life as a whole, with all your innumerable decisions, you are slowly turning your soul either into a heavenly creature or into a hellish creature."

Job's story is a powerful reminder of the human capacity to endure suffering with grace and maintain moral integrity in the face of adversity. Examples like Job have encouraged me to reflect on my resilience and integrity, offering hope and guidance during seasons when I have been navigating the complexities of life. They continually remind me that, even in the darkest moments, a steadfast commitment to faith, principles, and perseverance will lead to profound personal growth and serve as a beacon of light for others who are observing me.

While never desired, suffering and trials teach us to trust more deeply, experience God's presence more fully, refine our character, and cultivate resilience and hope. The path may be fraught with pain, but it is also lined with growth, discovery, and the potential for an enriched spiritual life. Let the stories of those who have walked this path before you offer hope and encouragement as you journey toward a deeper, more resilient faith.

In the crucible of suffering, hope and resilience are forged. Through enduring trials, we learn that our circumstances do not define us, nor do they have the final say in our lives. The stories of Job, Ron, and countless others who have walked through the valley of the shadow of death and emerged with a stronger faith serve as beacons of hope for all facing trials. These stories remind us that suffering is not the end but a chapter in a larger story of redemption and restoration.

Jonah
Heath Cole

"Now the Lord had prepared a great fish to swallow Jonah. And Jonah was in the belly of the fish three days and three nights."
Jonah 1:17

Stigler, Oklahoma. One of those small communities in eastern Oklahoma with two stoplights and a Walmart. Everyone knows everyone and I was no exception. Tragedy struck my home when I was only six years old. My father passed away unexpectedly, leaving my brother and I to be raised by our mother. Growing up, I vividly remember that Mom was a strong, Godly woman who never backed down from the devil. Her prayer life was a priority to her because she had two little boys to raise. She knew how hard it was going to be. And it was. Even at that young age, I felt like God was calling me to something greater than I could imagine. I wasn't sure exactly what He wanted from me, but I knew that He had a path for me to go down. As I began to get older and in my teenage years, I wanted to fit in with my friends more than I wanted to fit in with God. I began to run away from where God called me to go. Maybe I was scared of what I knew I was supposed to do. I don't know.

I can relate to Jonah. The Bible explains that God sent word to the prophet Jonah, saying *"Arise, go to Nineveh, that great city, and cry against it; for their wickedness is come up before me"* Jonah 1:2, KJV.

Nineveh was considered a large city and a great city. It was not called "great" simply because of its size, but due to the great amount of sin in it. Nineveh was a city with a reputation for violence and evil. So, when Jonah received instructions to go there, that was not what he had envisioned for his life. Maybe he was scared. I might have been, too. The Bible says that Jonah turned and went as far as possible in the opposite direction. Nineveh was 550 miles northeast of Israel, but he decided to head toward Tarshish, located on the coast of Spain some 2,500 miles to the west. Jonah found the first boat out of there and ran. Twice in Chapter 1, the Bible says that Jonah was trying to escape the *"presence of the Lord;"* the first time in verse 3 and also again in verse 10. The Bible is also clear that Jonah did not want Nineveh to experience God's forgiveness, Jonah 3:10, 4:1-2.

I know how Jonah felt when he ran. I paid a high price trying escape the presence of God. It is interesting that the prophet, who actually had conversations with God, thought that he could escape the presence of the Lord by physically moving from one place to another. Flashback to my life after high school. I was married and living a life filled with sin and addiction. My wife and I decided to move to another town, thinking that the guilt and conviction I felt would stop if we did. I thought that I could go somewhere where nobody knew me, and that God couldn't find me. I was desperate. Everything that could have gone wrong had gone wrong. I had been in jail, my children had been taken by the child protection services, and now I was making the choice to try and hide from God. Sin causes us to do some crazy things sometimes, but moving away from the presence of God is impossible. My choices only brought me deeper into sin. I was in the storm of my life, and it was rocking everything around me, while I just sat back and let it happen.

On the boat, the experienced sailors were scared for their life. They had never seen a storm like this. They began to panic by throwing the ship's cargo, and even their own luggage, overboard as the ship began to break apart. Meanwhile, Jonah seemed unaffected. He was sleeping while everything was crashing down around him. And like Jonah, I was responsible for the storm around me. I wasn't just hurting myself, but it was affecting my whole family. I didn't think I was hurting anyone but myself. My wife, my children, and my Mom were all being impacted, and I didn't even realize it. I was sleeping right through it. The whole time I was in my addiction, my sin was bringing a false sense of peace. I was asleep while everything was crashing down around me.

Because Jonah disobeyed God, he found himself in the center of a storm in the middle of the Mediterranean Sea. It wasn't long before the crew figured out that Jonah was to blame for the storm, and they now knew that they would have to make a hard, life or death decision. Ultimately, they threw Jonah overboard into the sea, and soon after that, he was swallowed by a large fish. Jonah found himself in the middle of a place that he could not get himself out of... the belly of a whale. Certainly not where Jonah had planned to spend the day.

I have a good friend who said that "sin will take you where you don't want to go, keep you longer than you want to stay, and cost you more than you can afford to pay." When we stay in sin, sin tightens its grip on us and makes it harder for us to get away. Consider this: If we never have our sins forgiven, then it will be our sins that will take us to hell.

In Chapter 2, Jonah cried out to God from the belly of the fish. *"From inside the fish Jonah prayed to the Lord his God. He said: "In my distress I called to the Lord, and he answered me. From deep in the realm of the dead I called for help, and you listened to my cry." And the Lord commanded the fish, and it vomited Jonah onto dry land"* NIV.

Jonah got a second chance. This time, he obeyed God. The city of Nineveh was infected by sin, but once Jonah proclaimed God's message, they immediately repented and cried out to God. *"Then God saw their works, that they turned from their evil way; and God relented from the disaster that He had said He would bring upon them, and He did not do it"* Jonah 3:10, KJV.

I also got a second chance and so did my family. God restored my family and I returned to the calling upon my life. I now pastor a small church in Shawnee, Oklahoma, a town that desperately needs God and His forgiveness. We are seeing the chains of bondage broken and the power of healing come to this community.

All because of *the belly of a fish.*

Jeremiah

Mark Topp

"The words of Jeremiah the son of Hilkiah, of the priests who were in
Anathoth in the land of Benjamin."
Jeremiah 1:1

Jeremiah is known as *the weeping Prophet*. Not really a tag you'd be proud of nowadays. We would want to be known as the powerful Prophet or the miracle working Prophet. Jeremiah was called this because his heart was tender and he witnessed awful things yet still kept his faith and trust in God. Jeremiah managed to work through the mental anguish and still kept his focus towards Heaven.

"My eyes fail from weeping, I am in torment within; my heart is poured out on the ground because my people are destroyed, because children and infants faint in the streets of the city" Lamentations 2:11, NIV.

I want to share my testimony with you and why Jeremiah's story inspires me and other men around the world. You see, I have witnessed my own set of painful things in my life. Here's a couple of examples. On the 1st of July in 2013, I became a father for the first time. The day before my grandmother died of cancer, after battling it so hard for so long, she didn't get a chance to meet her great-grandson and I was devastated. Lydia, my wife, and I had been so excited about becoming parents; we had so many plans and hopes and dreams for our baby. It was like a punch to the stomach and all the wind had been knocked out of me. It felt like I was at the start of an emotional whirlpool. Dealing with anger, doubts, and frustrations just to name a few feelings and emotions running through my mind. Reuben, my son, was born ten days over his due date. He was delivered by an emergency C-section and as a result of some complications during the C-section and labor process, Reuben suffered a traumatic brain injury. He was rushed from the operation room to Special Care Baby Unit and was then transferred to a major hospital 60 miles away.

"Oh, my anguish, my anguish! I writhe in pain. Oh, the agony of my heart! My heart pounds within me, I cannot keep silent" Jeremiah 4:19, NIV.

I was trying to process the loss of my grandmother and the traumatic labor my wife had gone through, and now to feeling this flood of emotions rushing through my tired body to care for this poor little boy that had just been born. I was spent physically and emotionally, and nearly spiritually. Lydia and I had been told the news that a Specialist Pediatrician doctor and nurse were coming on "blue lights" from Portsmouth to take Reuben to be given the specialist care and treatment he required. I picked up a Gideon's New Testament and Psalms that was in the hospital bedroom Lydia was in and I went to pray over my boy. I wanted to bless him as his Dad.

I walked into SCBU to see Reuben. As parents, Lydia and I had chosen two names for our boy: Malachi and Reuben, and we were favoring Malachi. I took one look at my boy and knew he wasn't going to be named Malachi, but his name would be *Reuben*. Reuben meaning the age-old saying "behold, a son." As I opened up the Gideon's New Testament and Psalms, I turned to Psalm 139 and read that wonder scripture over Reuben and blessed him. The maternity nurse left the room in tears as I did so.

Read and be encouraged:

*"You have searched me, Lord,
and you know me.*

154

JEREMIAH

You know when I sit and when I rise;
you perceive my thoughts from afar.
You discern my going out and my lying down;
you are familiar with all my ways.
Before a word is on my tongue
you, Lord, know it completely.
You hem me in behind and before,
and you lay your hand upon me.
Such knowledge is too wonderful for me,
too lofty for me to attain.
Where can I go from your Spirit?
Where can I flee from your presence?
If I go up to the heavens, you are there;
if I make my bed in the depths, you are there.
If I rise on the wings of the dawn,
if I settle on the far side of the sea,
even there your hand will guide me,
your right hand will hold me fast.
If I say, "Surely the darkness will hide me
and the light become night around me,"
even the darkness will not be dark to you;
the night will shine like the day,
for darkness is as light to you.
For you created my inmost being;
you knit me together in my mother's womb.
I praise you because I am fearfully and wonderfully made;
your works are wonderful,
I know that full well.
My frame was not hidden from you
when I was made in the secret place,
when I was woven together in the depths of the earth.
Your eyes saw my unformed body;
all the days ordained for me were written in your book
before one of them came to be.
How precious to me are your thoughts, God!
How vast is the sum of them!

Were I to count them,
they would outnumber the grains of sand—
when I awake, I am still with you.
If only you, God, would slay the wicked!
Away from me, you who are bloodthirsty!
They speak of you with evil intent;
your adversaries misuse your name.
Do I not hate those who hate you, Lord,
and abhor those who are in rebellion against you?
I have nothing but hatred for them;
I count them my enemies.
Search me, God, and know my heart;
test me and know my anxious thoughts.
See if there is any offensive way in me,
and lead me in the way everlasting" Psalm 139, NIV.

When the doctor arrived and the neonatal nurse started preparing Reuben for his journey in a special incubator bed that went in the ambulance to the hospital in Portsmouth, he took us into a family room, sat us down, and told us that Reuben was very poorly and that he couldn't guarantee that he would survive the next 24 hours. He asked us if we had named him yet and he encouraged us that we should, as it might be one of the only things we could do for our baby boy.

Together, we named him Reuben and prayed with him, and as he travelled in the ambulance to the hospital, we prayed together as a couple like we've never prayed before. With tears rolling down our faces, with our hearts poured out on the ground yet keeping our eyes on Jesus. It continued to be an emotional rollercoaster over the next ten days. Trips back and forth from hospitals visiting Reuben and visiting Lydia, and then spending five days up in Portsmouth Hospital when Lydia was well enough to travel to be with Reuben. Then, finally spending another four days back in Dorchester Hospital before we could take our boy home. Having Reuben and going through what we went through as a couple broke something in me. I had hardened my heart after growing up with my biological dad not being a part of my life and a stepdad that due to him and my Mum divorcing, wasn't a major part of my childhood growing up.

During this time, I cried like a tap had been released inside of me. I was broken and I needed Jesus to touch an area of my life that had been so guarded and protected. Having not had the most positive experiences with *Dads* in my life, I didn't want to screw up and be a disappointment to Reuben. I knew I needed Father God to lead me and guide me how to love Reuben like He loves me. I was so fearful that I couldn't be the Dad Reuben needed that I almost shut down my emotions towards him. God, through the power of the Holy Spirit, broke into that situation and gave me a capacity to love Reuben through the trials and tribulations we would face with the brain injury he suffered.

"My eyes flow and do not cease, Without interruption, Till the Lord from heaven Looks down and sees" Lamentations 3:49-50

Reuben has a Grade 2 HIE diagnosis. His brain was starved of oxygen, suffers with Global Development Delay, and an Autism diagnosis to cap it all off. We thought God had done a miracle. Our boy was home and he started hitting milestones and development markers then all of a sudden, it just all slowed down and he began to get frustrated and we needed help. Raising children is a privilege; it's rewarding and it's tough sometimes. Raising a child with Additional/Special Needs is next level. Before Reuben was born, I was working in management for a large pharmaceutical business and had experienced some bullying at work which had caused me to have a short period of depression that lasted for around 6-8 months. I was signed off sick from work. Everyday life was affected, even getting out of bed was a struggle most mornings and finding joy in anything was incredibly hard. I thank God for Lydia, my incredible wife, who supported me in the early years of our marriage through this and I thank God that He helped me in this situation.

When Lydia told me the wonderful news that we were expecting our 2nd child, I was delighted but there was a niggling feeling inside of me that was worrying me. What if the next baby has the same experiences as Reuben? What if all our hopes, dreams, and ambitions for our next child get blown out of the water again? As Joel, our 2nd boy, was born in August of 2017, God had to shift something within me as I had started to guard my heart from feeling the paternal love I needed to show Joel. As a way of protecting myself from being hurt, I guess. I knew it wasn't right and during a real and raw time of prayer, the Holy Spirit touched my life and changed my heart. The guard that I had placed up came crashing down.

Another testimony I want to share with you. As a couple, Lydia and I lead a church in Dorchester in the UK. We have two amazing boys both with additional needs and life is hard sometimes, and God is good all the time. We have seen God work in Reuben's life in incredible ways as the doctors said he wouldn't be able to do much yet he astounds us every day. Both Reuben and Joel have been used by God to bring qualities out of us that we didn't know God had gifted us with. I have been able to train alongside my church ministry as a First Aider for Mental Health Instructor and have a passion for supporting church congregations, especially men in their mental health.

When we read Scripture and see these mighty men of God, we can easily focus on the highlight reel of their lives, or ministry. Jeremiah reminds us that we, as men, all face battles, external and internal ones. However, if we keep our eyes fixed on Jesus, the Bible reminds us that the battle belongs to the Lord. The Lord fights our battles and if He is for us, who should stand against us! Whatever your struggle is, keep your eyes fixed to Heaven. Allow the Holy Spirit to minister to those areas that have been guarded and trust in The Lord.

"Through the Lord's mercies we are not consumed, Because His compassions fail not. They are new every morning; Great is Your faithfulness. "The Lord is my portion," says my soul, "Therefore I hope in Him!" Lamentations 3:22-24

Blind Bartimaeus

D. Lawrence Elliott

"Now they came to Jericho. As He went out of Jericho with His disciples and a great multitude, blind Bartimaeus, the son of Timaeus, sat by the road begging." Mark 10:46

A Beggar or a Believer

When it comes to your relationship with God, are you a Beggar or a Believer? The story of **Blind Bartimaeus,** son of Timaeus, is a powerful narrative found in all four of the Gospels. We will concentrate on the Gospel of Mark, Mark 10:46-52, NKJV. The scripture says:

"Now they came to Jericho. As He went out of Jericho with His disciples and a great multitude, blind Bartimaeus, the son of Timaeus, sat by the road begging."

Notice that Mark mentions a large crowd walking with Jesus. Jesus is less than two weeks before the Passover and the Cross. Mark gives us the blind man's name, *Bartimaeus*, the son of Timaeus. His life was marked by darkness, both physically and spiritually. He was an outcast, marginalized by society, and reduced to begging for survival. There are two theological thoughts concerning his name; when we look up the Greek meaning of "Timaeus," we discover the word means "honor." Bartimaeus could have been the son of a socially significant man of the region, someone well-known. The other thought comes from Matthew Henry's Commentary, "...*Bartimaeus, that is, the son of Timaeus;* which, some think, signifies *the son of a blind man;*" So, he could have been "the blind son of a blind father."

A beggar is one who makes a living, or survives, by asking for something they had no part in earning. And they do not know if they will get it or not. They would sit just outside the city gates where the most significant amount of traffic would come by for them to seek alms with their cloak spread out to catch any coins tossed their way.

"And when he heard that it was Jesus of Nazareth, he began to cry out and say, "Jesus, Son of David, have mercy on me!" vs. 47.

By addressing Jesus as the "Son of David," Bartimaeus affirmed his belief that Jesus was the **Messiah** (see 2 Samuel 7:14–16). He believed in his heart who Jesus was. A believer is fully and totally convinced, and Bartimaeus was. He has made up his mind that this is God Almighty. This is the one who has the power to change his life and heal him. And the crowd tried to cancel him.

"Then many warned him to be quiet, but he cried out all the more, "Son of David, have mercy on me!" vs 48.

The crowd gave sharp disapproval. The people one would expect to help intentionally sought to shut him up. But he screamed ever the louder, over, and over, "JESUS... SON OF DAVID... HAVE MERCY ON ME!" Bartimaeus decided he had one shot; he gave it all his might, power, and strength. The cool thing is that over all the noise of the crowd, Jesus still heard Bartimaeus. His persistent faith breaks his spiritual blindness.

"So Jesus stood still and commanded him to be called. Then they called the blind man, saying, "Be of good cheer. Rise, He is calling you" vs 49.

Desperation and perspiration grabs Jesus's attention. Jesus heard the desperate plea of a desperate man over the clamor of the crowd! He, who commanded the heavens and the Earth into existence, makes a command, it happens.

"And throwing aside his garment, he rose and came to Jesus" vs. 50.

That cloak was not just an item of clothing. It was an essential item of clothing; a cloak defined him as a beggar. It was like his permission slip to be sitting there asking for money. It was his identity. By discarding it, he symbolically let go of his old life, his past, embracing the possibility of transformation. He laid aside the weight and the sin which so easily beset him, Hebrews 12:1. Bartimaeus was a believer; he took a step of faith.

"So Jesus answered and said to him, "What do you want Me to do for you?" vs. 51.

What a strange question to ask a blind man. But Jesus never asked a foolish question in His life. Jesus wanted to hear it from the man's lips. Jesus wanted him to "ask, so that he might receive."

"The blind man said to Him, "Rabboni, that I may receive my sight."

Bartimaeus sees Jesus as "Rabboni," Master... Teacher! He saw Jesus as the Potter, and he was the clay. Jesus was the Teacher, and he was the student.

"Then Jesus told him, "Go your way; your faith has made you well." *And immediately, he received his sight and followed Jesus on the road"* vs. 52.

Bartimaeus had the kind of faith that pleases God, a wholehearted trust in Jesus. In Hebrews 11:6, NKJV, we are told:

"But without faith it is impossible to please Him, for he who comes to God must believe that He is and that He is a rewarder of those who diligently seek Him."

His healing went beyond physical eyesight; it touched his soul. His faith had made him whole. Tucked neatly away at the very end of that chapter, and easily overlooked are six words:

"... and followed Jesus on the road."

What way? Where? I like to think that Bartimaeus followed Jesus to the Cross; he had become a follower of Christ.

There was a time when I was blinded and dulled to my sin after coming back from overseas in the Army. I was spat on and ostracized for the uniform I wore. I took that uniform off, and threw it and the medals away. I was a blind beggar man in my spirit. I found myself sitting on the outskirts of a bottle of whiskey. I had the all-too-human unwillingness to recognize the barriers that kept me from remembering God, myself, and others. I would not say I liked the world and everyone around me.

I was admitted to the Veterans Administration Dom in Temple, Texas, for alcoholism and drug use. My mind was tormented with Post Traumatic Stress Disorder, and I was suicidal. I was a social outcast, even in some churches. You see, I had been a Pastor! A fallen shepherd of His sheep. I cried out in desperation! People thought, "Jesus will not help him! He is already too far gone! Curse God and die!"

In my desperation, I screamed, "Jesus! Jesus, have mercy on me!" Jesus stopped for me! He called me by name. He healed me... my mind, my body, and my spirit, and made me whole. Ever since that day, I have followed Jesus in the Way.

My question today is, "Are you a beggar or a believer?" Do you come to Jesus begging, "Jesus, if it be Your will... Lord, if it pleases You...?"

I don't know what you may see in your life today, the storm you are heading into or the season of pain and struggle you have been living in; whatever it is you are believing for and whatever it is you need, Jesus already paid for it for you 2000 years ago on the Cross.

BLIND BARTIMAEUS

You do not have to wonder if it is in His will; you do not have to beg and plead. Just take a step in faith today. Stand by His Word! His Promises. And say, "I am a believer! Even though I may not see it right now, even though I may not feel it right now, I will thank You until I do, in Your Mighty Name, Amen!"

We need to release our old identities, sins, and worldly attachments. When we encounter Jesus, we must let go of what hinders us.

Jesus is standing and asking you today, *"What do you want me to do for you?"*

Moses

Anonymous

"Moshe said to God, "Who am I, that I should go to Pharaoh and lead the people of Isra'el out of Egypt?" Exodus 3:11, CJB

Moses, or his Hebrew name *Moshe*, was born during a time of spiritual chaos and upheaval. Pharaoh's astrologers prophesied that they had seen in the stars that there was a Jewish savior that would come to free the Hebrews from slavery. Pharaoh became angry and commanded and decreed that all newborn Hebrew/Israelite boys be drowned in the Nile River to ensure that this "savior" would not enter the world. It is said that Yokheved gave birth to Moses, or Moshe, three months prematurely. She hid the baby until what would have been her ninth month of pregnancy, so the Egyptians would not take him from her and kill him. When she could hide him no longer, she wrapped him in warm clothing and put him inside of a papyrus basket and coated it with clay and tar to protect him, hiding Moshe amongst the reeds on the riverbank. Why would she do this knowing they were adamant about killing all newborn Hebrew boys? She knew the location the basket would be placed would eventually be seen of Pharoah's daughter, Bithiah (Bityah), or at least her servants.

We are not privy to any scripture that provides us with solid information that Yahweh had spoken directly to Yokheved to carry out this heroic and selfless act, but nonetheless, she completed it with success.

The Torah and the Bible both give reference to Moses' (Moshe's) father as being that of a Levite, and that Yokheved was a daughter of a Levite; therefore, marking Moses (Moshe) in the lineage of the Levitical Priesthood.

"A man from the family of Levi took a woman also descended from Levi as his wife. When she conceived and had a son, upon seeing what a fine child he was, she hid him for three months. When she could no longer hide him, she took a papyrus basket, coated it with clay and tar, put the child in it and placed it among the reeds on the riverbank. His sister stood at a distance to see what would happen to him" Exodus 2:1-4, CJB.

Nowhere in Scripture do we see Moses's (Moshe's) father Amram being active in his life, or in the lives of his brother, Aaron (Aharon) or his sister Miriam (Miryam). He all but disappears and does not have a mention as to his role in the life of Moses (Moshe). He was only noted in the genealogy of the Hebrews and that he was, indeed, their father.

"Amram married Yokheved his father's sister, and she bore him Aharon and Moshe. 'Amram lived to be 137 years old" Exodus 6:20, CJB.

In ancient times, especially in Hebrew/Jewish custom and tradition, the next kinsman in the family would marry the widowed wife of the family. This would secure and stabilize the bloodline throughout the generations. In this case, Amram is said to have married his father's sister, Yokheved. It is not clear in Scripture if she was a widow, but this would usually be the one of the reasons for marrying along these lines. Nevertheless, we are shown that he is the father of Moses (Moshe), Aaron (Aharon), and Miriam (Miryam).

"The name of 'Amram's wife was Yokheved the daughter of Levi, who was born to Levi in Egypt; and she bore to 'Amram Aharon, Moshe and their sister Miryam" Numbers 26:59.

Fathers are an extremely important part of their children's lives. Whether they are physically in their lives, deceased, or even what many coin "the sperm donor," a father is who provides identity for his children, especially his sons. Being the son of Kohath (K'hat) son of Levi, Amram was evidently raised in the order of the priesthood. His children would have been trained along the same lines as well, yet Moses (Moshe) was a baby when he was sent out to the palace of Pharoah. His identity was, in essence, stripped from him in order to save his life. He was raised as an Egyptian, in the ways and spiritual practices of his adoptive family. Their religion was polytheistic, meaning they served multiple gods. The Torah and the Bible notes that Moses (Moshe) lived to be 120 years old and that he was around 80 years old when he met Yahweh on the Mountain of Sinai to find out who was the One True God of his ancestors, his birth family.

"Moshe was eighty years old and Aharon eighty-three when they spoke to Pharaoh" Exodus 7:7

We can gather from his life's timeline that he had spent 40 years of his life being learned in Egyptian life and spirituality. It is said that he spent the next 40 years in the desert, where he met his wife Zipporah (Tzipporah) and had his first sons, Gershom and Eli'ezer. The next 40 years of his life would be spent freeing the Hebrews from Egyptian bondage and wandering in the wilderness with the children of Israel in search of the Promised Land, of which he would not be able to enter.

One can only imagine the inner thoughts of this man who was saved from death as an infant, but reared in a false religion not able to be trained and raised up in the priesthood of the Levites and the religion of his forefathers. Then, to have the truth of his existence revealed to him only to flee to the desert for 40 years to be met by the One True God, Yahweh, who would *send him back* to free His people. Though Moses (Moshe) may not have known exactly who he was, Yahweh knew him intimately.

"Before I formed you in the womb, I knew you; before you were born, I separated you for myself. I have appointed you to be a prophet to the nations" Jeremiah 1:5, CJB.

When Yahweh has a plan for a man's life, He will move Heaven and Earth to get you to your expected destination.

"For I know what plans I have in mind for you,' says Adonai, 'plans for well-being, not for bad things; so that you can have hope and a future" Jeremiah 29:11

Men of Yahweh, Sons of Purpose, you were born into this world with your gifts, your calling, and your purpose already predestined and established by your Creator, your ABBA Father in Heaven. Though Moses (Moshe) may not have known his biological father, and was raised by an adoptive father of differing beliefs and practices, he was met by his ABBA Father, the One who created him and set forth a trajectory that would change his entire life, and the world as we know it today.

No matter what position you may find yourself in, no matter what has happened to you as a child, a teenager, or even as an adult, know and trust that Yahweh has a path set for your life, as well. He sees your beginning from your end. He intimately knows the people, places, and situations you will encounter and face in this thing called "life," and He will use it ALL to bring you to your expected end. He is a GOOD Father, our ABBA Father, and we are His beloved sons.

"Now because you are sons, God has sent forth into our hearts the Spirit of his Son, the Spirit who cries out, "Abba!" (that is, "Dear Father!")" Galatians 4:6.

Barnabas

Gabriel Daniels

"As they ministered to the Lord and fasted, the Holy Spirit said, "Now separate to Me Barnabas and Saul for the work to which I have called them." Acts 13:2

W hen I was approached to write a devotional about various sons of purpose in the Bible that God used for extraordinary purposes, Barnabas was not my first choice. I wanted to write about Moses, Joseph, David (the man after God's heart), Paul, etc., but all those heroes of faith were already chosen by other writers. But, as I scanned down the list, I felt the Holy Spirit nudging me to choose Barnabas. I did not realize why until the very moment I began to write my devotional on Barnabas. Just like Barnabas, God has given me a heart to encourage others on their journey. A close friend of mine, Joon, said to me, and I quote: "You're so responsive and supportive" and I replied, "Thank you, brother! The Lord gets all the glory! I try to be God's hands and feet! And so many people, including you, have encouraged me when I needed it the most. So, why was Barnabas, whose real name is Joseph, nicknamed Barnabas, which means "Son of Encouragement," an encourager? Stay with me and I will tell you his amazing story and how my story ties into his!

Barnabas was born a Levite from Cyprus and as I mentioned, his real name was Joseph. He was given the nickname of Barnabas by the apostles, meaning *Son of Encouragement*, because he loved to encourage others. What does an encourager do? An encourager helps others by giving them what they need, or speaking motivational words to keep them from quitting. An encourager always seeks the best for others and wants to see them do well. I believe I am gifted with the same spirit of an encourager just like Barnabas. My journey to be an encourager started at birth.

I was born in Monrovia, Liberia to a mother, a descendant of free African slaves from America, who returned to Africa and established the first independent nation in Africa, Liberia. My father left before I was born and so I grew up with my mother and my beloved grandmother, Hannah Pratt, who passed away in 2005. Growing up as a fatherless child, I always desired to have a father; I did not realize that God had always been a father to me. I came to the United States for the first time in 1986 at the age of four years old and it would be the first time that I would meet my dad. I returned to my birth country of Liberia and soon after, a civil war started and engulfed the entire nation. During the Civil War, I saw my first beheaded body at the tender age of seven years old, and the atrocities and carnage that I experienced, unknowingly to me, led to my calling of being an encourager just like Barnabas. You see, when you experienced what I had to endure as a child, you learned at a very young age that God is always the *Rock* at the bottom. With that mindset, you begin to trust in the faithfulness of God, and the Lord, through His Holy Spirit, changes you into an individual who wants the best for humanity just like He does! Usually, when people endure what I have endured, it results in cynical and erratic behavior. But with the help of God, I saw what hatred and violence can do to a nation; so instead of hate, I chose to encourage. I chose to uplift. I chose to motivate. I chose to love, and see people as God sees them.

So, although the Bible does not tell us much about Barnabas' early life, I infer that something dramatic must have taken place to help facilitate his journey to becoming a "Son of Encouragement". In Acts 4:36-37, the Bible briefly tells us that Barnabas belonged to the tribe of Levi. Levites are the tribe chosen by God to perform sanctuary services in the Jewish temple. Being a Levite most likely meant that Barnabas was a teacher of law in a synagogue in Cyprus. Barnabas was always a very generous man as in Acts 4:37, it speaks about him selling a piece of land and bringing all the proceeds to the apostles. As a child, I grew up in church and was taught by my grandmother and mom about God and Our precious Savior, Jesus Christ. I always had a heart for God and doing His will but unlike Barnabas, I had a journey of a Prodigal. I left the path of the Lord and ventured into exploring the ways and sins of the world. Yet, my heart of encouragement never departed my character as I continued to encourage others even when I was not living for God, or in the right standing with Him.

As Barnabas, I am also a very generous individual and love helping others. It's a blessing that the Lord blessed me with a wife that shared the same generous heart as mine and we both are cheerful givers. As our Lord Jesus said, *it is more blessed to give than to receive.* The most telling thing about Barnabas' story for me is the fact that he was the one who recommended Paul to the apostles. Okay, pause right here! The Holy Spirit led me to search for the apostle that the Lord appeared to in a dream and told him to go and pray for Saul after his dramatic and life-changing encounter with Our Lord, Jesus Christ on the road to Damascus. Quick reference, you see Saul persecuted early Christians as he was zealous for the law of the Pharisees and believed in his heart that Christians were not obeying God's laws. Well, that mindset all changed when he met Jesus on the road to Damascus. In Acts 9: 1-20, the Bible tells us about Saul's amazing encounter with Jesus and how the Lord appeared to Saul and asked him why he was persecuting Him. This amazing encounter led Saul to lose his sight for a moment and he had to be led into the city of Damascus.

While Saul was at a house in Damascus, the Lord appeared to Ananias and told him to go to the house where Saul was staying to pray for him. So, stick with me, Ananias obeyed the Lord and prayed for Saul after a few objections, so I am thinking about why Ananias was not the one to vouch for Saul who became Paul to the apostles when they were hesitant about welcoming him into their brotherhood. I have no idea why, but it is very interesting that it was Barnabas who vouched for Saul who, at that time, had become Paul. This, for me, exemplifies the true characteristics of Barnabas' heart and why he was nicknamed a name which means *Son of Encouragement.* Barnabas, just like Jesus, always seeks to see the best in humanity, despite all their flaws.

In Acts 11:24, we see that Barnabas was also a preacher of the Gospel. The early church leaders in Jerusalem sent Barnabas to Antioch to strengthen the members of the faith. He encouraged them to continue to trust and have faith in the Lord and many people came to believe in the Lord. The Bible shows us that Barnabas was a great preacher because he was truly a good man, who truly desired to do God's will and be God's hands and feet. He was filled with the Holy Spirit and pleasing God was his desire. I started to become bolder with sharing the Gospel of Our Lord, Jesus Christ. I am led more by the Spirit now than my flesh as I trust in the Lord's sanctification process.

Early on in my walk with the Lord, I did not show God's grace as I would argue with non-believers instead of showing empathy and compassion while I shared the Good News of Jesus. I desire to be more like Barnabas in my approach to sharing the Gospel and live a life that truly pleases God and shows the world God's grace and love through how I live and love God's people. My desire is for everyone that I encounter to see Christ in me and most importantly, come to know Jesus for themselves. Barnabas also brought Paul to Antioch after preaching the Gospel. In Acts 11:25-25, we find Barnabas going to get Paul who escaped to Tarsus when adversaries of his were conspiring and plotting to kill him. Barnabas got Paul and spent an entire year working together sharing the Gospel. One of the fondest and most transformative periods in my life was when I did a study plan with my godfather, Jim Wright, called *Paul, Barnabas, Timothy Men's Devotional Study*. The study comes with a workbook, and you get to spend time with a mentor and explore Scripture, your personal life story, and your mentor who disciples you in the way of the Lord.

In the study, *Paul* represents that person in your life who mentors, leads, and directs you. This is the man who comes alongside you to disciple you along the road of faith and life. This is someone who has traveled further down the road of faith and life than you. While *Barnabas* is someone who encourages you and holds you accountable in your faith and life. This is a mutual friendship, or what's called in the world of spiritual formation, a "spiritual friendship." And finally, *Timothy* is that man *you* help guide along the road of faith and life. This is generally someone who has not traveled as far as you have in your walk with

Christ. Such a man is marked (or should be) by an eagerness to grow in his relationship with Christ and is humble and teachable enough to receive what you must share and to interact with you on the things of faith and life.

In the study, I was Timothy and Mr. Jim Wright was Paul and Barnabas as he mentored and encouraged me to continue my maturity in the Lord. I learned his life story and he learned mine and the time we spent together doing the study drew us closer together that I asked him to be my godfather. Jim is now in my life forever and I can call on him whenever I have questions, or need prayer or advice. Jim also runs a Men's group at Grace Covenant Church in Chantilly, VA. God has used those groups of men to help nurture and encourage me as I trust and follow Our Lord, Jesus Christ. I truly believe it is so important to have a band of brothers who are all chasing after God with a desire to know and please Him. Mentorship is paramount for spiritual growth, so please seek to be mentored or mentor others.

In Acts 11: 26, we also see that Barnabas, through his ministry with Paul, taught believers in Antioch how to imitate Our Precious Savior, Jesus in their words, actions, and overall conduct. Barnabas and Paul were so much like Christ that early "Christ-followers" were called *Christians* for the first time in Antioch. God has called me to a group of men that I shared Scripture with daily and encourage them to continue our walk with the Lord. I, too, like Barnabas, teach the importance of imitating Christ in all we do. I also teach them the importance of resting in Jesus's finished works. I believe many believers of Christ, including myself, don't know, or ever rest in, the Lord. When I say rest, I mean being completely satisfied with the Lord and surrendering and trusting Him completely. We can only accomplish this by spending time with God in the Secret Place. The Secret Place is the place you set apart to meet with God daily. I have seen growth in my spiritual maturity the more time I spend with the Lord in the Secret Place.

Another great quality of Barnabas was that he was a man of great integrity. In Acts 11-27-30, the Bible tells us that when a great famine broke out in Jerusalem, the early believers chose to send aid through Barnabas and Paul. This choice signified how much the believers trusted

Barnabus and Paul and that they would deliver the aid as intended. Integrity is a requirement for any Christ follower and just like Barnabas, I strive to live a life of integrity by being truthful and honest in everything. It is also important to note that Barnabas was set apart by God and had a special calling on his life.

In Acts 13:2-5, the Holy Spirit separated Barnabas and Paul for a special assignment as missionaries, while they prayed and fasted with other believers in Antioch. After being ordained by the laying on of hands, Barnabus and Paul left on their first missionary journey together. I believe that the Lord has set me apart for ministry as well. As I wait on the Lord's timing, I am encouraged to continue striving to please God in all I do. My desire is intimacy with God and a real relationship. I want to have a heart that desires to please and serve God. I want to lead others to God through ministering to them and caring for their needs. I want to serve others just as our Lord, Jesus Christ, was a servant leader.

Finally, like all of us, Barnabas did have a flaw. We see his flaw in Galatians 2:13 which tells of how Barnabas was influenced by Peter to avoid eating with the Gentiles while in Galatia. This was hypocrisy since Barnabas knew that Jesus came as a Savior for the whole world and not only the Jews. Barnabas was prone to human weaknesses, just like each of us. Although Barnabas was a man of integrity, he, just like all of us, had sinful characteristics. However, our weaknesses should always point us to the Cross and the feet of Jesus. The Lord is the lover of our souls and Scripture says, *"He that begins a good work in us will see it to the end."*

To conclude, the life of Barnabas was a life that exemplified what true Christian mentorship looks like. He was the only one who encouraged Paul and believed in him when no one else trusted him after his conversion. Barnabas also provided Paul with opportunities to minister in Antioch and traveled with Paul on their first missionary journey. Barnabas was even willing to let Paul advance as he moved on to encourage the next mentee who needed his support—Mark.

Barnabas lived a life pulled out for others. His life sought to advance the Kingdom of God and God's righteousness. And for both Paul and

Mark, Barnabas did an excellent job in preparing them for ministry. Paul ended up being more prominent than Barnabas and by the end of their missionary journey in Acts 15:2, they were no longer referred to as Barnabas and Paul. Instead, they were called Paul and Barnabas.

Finally, like Barnabas, we, too, can be a source of encouragement to others in their journey through life. And by God's grace, we can point them to Jesus and help them grow in ministry, on a job, in our families, through the community, and in other different facets of life. At the end of his life and years later, Barnabas is known as an *encourager*. What will your life reflect, as in the others, after God calls you home?

Jude

Mike Leichner

"Jude, the servant of Jesus Christ, and brother of James, to them that are sanctified by God the Father, and preserved in Jesus Christ, and called: Mercy unto you, and peace, and love, be multiplied." Jude 1:1

I see Jude as a hero of the faith. To me, a hero is a man with convictions. The man Jude was a half-brother of Jesus. He doesn't try to make that an element in his life; he calls himself a servant of Jesus Christ. He was a fighter, a strong preacher, and a defender of the faith. He spoke boldly that believers should see to it that we would earnestly contend for the faith that was delivered unto the saints.

"But ye, beloved, building up yourselves on your most holy faith, praying in the Holy Ghost" Jude 20.

Jude had lived in the same home as Jesus. He undoubtedly saw firsthand the faith sustained in Jesus. A faith that was so strong that demon spirits had no power. Faith so strong that nothing was impossible. Sickness and disease could not remain in the face of that faith. Jude wanted to make sure that this strong faith was not lost, or hindered, or forgotten in the lives of Jesus' followers. Jude thundered against the wickedness of his day. He referred to those who crept in denying Jesus Christ, the angels who demonically rebelled, and the rebellious of Sodom and Gomorrah as filthy dreamers who defile the flesh, despise dominion, and speak evil of dignitaries. That's a strong defender and a man of great convictions!

For its size there is probably no book in the Bible that packs a greater faith punch than the 25 verses that comprise the book written by the Man of God, Jude. I love Jude, he was an *alpha male*. He preached against weak-kneed Christianity and false teachings. Definitely, Jude was a man of convictions. A man without convictions is no real Man of God at all! We might say today that Jude was "all in!" The main theme of this book is "faith on another level." This is another level in God, in the realm of the Spirit. This faith releases the ability to bypass the natural life into the supernatural. So many times in the Body of Christ, we settle or stop moving forward at salvation. This in spite of the Word that the Bible plainly declares that we are to leave the foundations of the faith and push on into higher heights and deeper depths.

"So let us stop going over the basic teachings about Christ again and again. Let us go on instead and become mature in our understanding. Surely we don't need to start again with the fundamental importance of repenting from evil deeds and placing our faith in God. You don't need further instruction about baptisms, the laying on of hands, the resurrection of the dead, and eternal judgment" Hebrews 6:1-2, NLT.

Most men will relate to that by just applying it to our natural life. You start with the basics which you must have but then you push on. All manner of athletes, and men in the military—we push ourselves to limits and then go beyond that to be champions! This is not something new, it was taught by the Apostles with passion. Those preachers had a "move it" spirit on their lives. They were men with Biblical conviction. Most Holy Faith is a contagious life when it comes to things of the Spirit. You can read much more on this subject in my book *Most Holy Faith*. Too many times, we find ourselves like Peter in the Courtyard, warming ourselves by the fire—not in the Fire. Close by, next to it, close to the river of God's Holy Ghost, just not in it. This could be due to our raising of traditions over and over, our lack of knowledge, or even fear of the unknown. It is said that blood is thicker than water, but I am of the consensus that tradition is thicker than blood. I've seen it and I have also experienced it.

"Well then, what shall I do? I will pray in the spirit, and I will also pray in words I understand. I will sing in the spirit, and I will also sing in words I understand" 1 Corinthians 14:15, NLT.

In this scripture verse, the Apostle Paul emphasized and made it very clear what we can and should do to keep our faith strong and to stand in Truth with conviction. "What then shall I do? I will pray in the Spirit and I will pray with words of understanding." This is powerful!

"And the Holy Spirit helps us in our weakness. For example, we don't know what God wants us to pray for. But the Holy Spirit prays for us with groanings that cannot be expressed in words. And the Father who knows all hearts knows what the Spirit is saying, for the Spirit pleads for us believers in harmony with God's own will" Romans 8:26-27, NLT.

"For he who speaks in a tongue does not speak to men but to God, for no one understands him; however, in the spirit he speaks mysteries" 1 Corinthians 14:2, NKJV.

This was prophesied in Isaiah 28:12 yet they would not hear. Can you imagine that? Traditions can deafen the spiritual ear. They would not hear. What we can hear are principles, foundational doctrines, and church treatises. Do we need all of those? Yes, of course, they are foundational. But never to the extent that they override the entirety of the Word. I had been raised in a wonderful church by wonderful Godly people. Even so, I went my own way, not God's. I was in the Marine Corp on my way to Boot Camp two months following my seventeenth birthday. The depths of my sinful life was far reaching, but that's not my story. Following my Honorable Discharge, I came home. One year later, Jesus picked me up, saved me, and set my feet on a path of Godly purpose! I came from a family with generations of ministry, so it wasn't hard to see and accept my Call. My brothers and I traveled every week-end in music ministry until God's Holy Word burned in me and I was preaching in the singing concerts. God dealt with me in profound ways and soon, in response to Him, I had resigned from my job, sold my house, and packed my wife and two young children into a pickup truck pulling a 21' travel trailer. We were in revivals all over the nation, 49 weeks every year. I HAD DIVINE PURPOSE, but it wasn't complete.

Three and a half years into our travels, we began to feel a lack, a void; my wife called it as she went into prayer and fasting. It wasn't long and she was baptized in the Holy Ghost with the evidence of speaking in tongues. She had no idea what had occurred in her life, only that it was most definitely God. There is so much more to the story. There were incredible supernatural acts of God that led me right to the River of His Holy Spirit. I found myself in waters to swim in (Ezekiel 47:5) speaking in a spiritual language and so wonderfully changed! I was no longer acting out of my own wisdom—I had access to God's wisdom on a new level. Mysteries in the Spirit were released, I Corinthians 14:2. There is a release in your spirit as Jude was telling us. The Holy Ghost immediately becomes active. The language of the Holy Ghost is brought from Heaven.

This is a supernatural language that God wants us to have! The benefits are unparalleled and powerful! It is God the Holy Ghost that creates every single word in your mouth. It is the Spirit of God super imposing Himself upon the Spirit of man as we release Him by faith. We have enhanced purpose because we are armed with powerful gifts. The Holy Ghost searches your heart and prays the mind of God concerning you, bringing it into existence. Think of it! Natural law that is in subjection to supernatural wisdom of God. Among man there has never existed a language that carries the vocabulary to express the hidden wisdom, mysteries, and secret things of God, (I Corinthians 2, read the entire chapter).

Jude wrote to Believers. He identified them as having been *called*. He said *set apart*. He also said *preserved in Christ*. I relate to that! He again exhorted us to contend for the faith, be diligent, fight, be strong, and do it earnestly. It is a blessing, a joy, and a positive privilege. Again, I relate! Then, in verse 20, we are told to be "building ourselves up on our most holy faith, praying in the Holy Ghost." I relate to that! Surely, we should all take this power packed book to heart and respond with expectation to do as the Amplified version of verse 20 says:

"But you, beloved, build yourselves up on [the foundation of] your most holy faith [continually progress, rise like an edifice higher and higher], pray in the Holy Spirit."

We will rise higher and higher! We will be built up and continually progress!

Simon Peter

Ulysses James Chaney

"And Simon Peter answered and said, Thou art the Christ, the Son of the living God." Matthew 16:16

Among the things I love about reading and studying the sacred Word is learning about, and from, the lives and experiences of those men and women mentioned in the scriptures. One of the first things I have learned to recognize is they did not have a Bible to guide them; however, they had something I strive to have daily—a relationship with God that helped them navigate the world in which they lived. One such biblical personality was a fisherman named *Simon Peter*. Peter's walk with and in Christ reflects the grace of God, towards him, to become who God called him to be.

"And He saith unto them, follow me, and I will make you fishers of men" Matthew 4:19, KJV.

Considering the scriptural life of Peter, one could discern the process of him transitioning from a fisherman into *a fisher of men*. Starting off, he was a husband, a brother, and likely a partner and friend to other fishermen. Arguably, Peter was among the first called by Jesus to become a disciple; and he was part of what many refer to as the inner circle of Christ, which included James and John. In Christ, Peter was a rock or stone depending on the translation; however, in his humanity, he was flawed, even after receiving the gift of the Holy Ghost, but God's grace yet prevailed.

Looking at the gospels, the Book of Acts, and considering what the apostle Paul wrote regarding him, I find Peter's life and Christian experience one we can learn from. When called, Peter was going about life; according to Matthew chapter 4, he and his brother were working when Jesus called him (them). Receiving the calling, Peter dropped everything to follow the Lord, and witnessed, with few exceptions, everything Christ said and did. And yet, he had epic failures in character and was scolded several times by the Lord.

Thinking about it, Peter asked to meet Christ as He walked on water; only to be distracted and sink, Matthew 14: 28-31. Believing he wasn't worthy, Peter initially resisted Jesus washing his feet. Unwisely, Peter objected to Jesus' assignment being carnal minded, Matthew 16:21-23. Although with James and John, Peter was called out for falling asleep, when he should have been praying, Mark 14:32-42. In defense of the Lord, he cut the ear off a servant of the high priest, John 18:10-11. Then later, denied knowing Jesus, John 18:15-27.

In Acts chapter 10, Peter felt the need to defend the work of God to his brethren. And Paul confronted him for hypocrisy, Galatians 2:11-13. These are just a few of his mishaps; and despite these, other shortcomings, and chastisements, Peter was yet called, chosen, and the grace of God was upon him to become and be an apostle.

In my humanity, I can identify with Peter and his struggles. Like Peter, I was doing life when I received my calling from the Lord and have experienced things in God, that some believers might question the validity of. I have served and walked alongside true men and women of God; being present to witness the manifold blessings of God and the manifestation of the gifts of His Spirit. Although I am a teacher, I have preached the Gospel and His gifts have flowed through me also. And yet, I have failed in my walk at times and have been chastised by the Lord. I did not, and often still, believe I am not worthy of the vocation for which I am called. Jesus has caught me sleeping when I should have been praying. In my walk, I have spoken and done harmful things (intentionally and unintentionally) to people, felt defensive of the work of God through me, and have been a hypocrite. And although I have never verbally denied knowing Christ, my behaviors could have suggested it. And yet His love, mercy, compassion, and grace prevail, and I am yet holding on.

Peter was graced to transition from being a fisherman to a fisher of men; and further from being a disciple to an apostle. Despite all his fallacies, he had a revelation of who Jesus was, and was given the keys to the Kingdom, Matthew 16:15-20, and was instructed to not only feed the sheep, but to strengthen the brethren. Once filled with the Spirit, he spoke boldly of the things of God, established the first church and its administrators, and walked in the promise of Christ doing greater things, John 14:12; Acts 3:1-8; Acts 5:15; etc.

When I think of Peter, I remember the hymn "A Charge to Keep I Have". In addition to being called, chosen, and gifted of the Spirit of God, Peter had a charge spoken to him directly according to the scripture, John 21:15-17. And Jesus prayed for his conversion, so that he could strengthen others in Christ, Luke 22:32.

Just like Peter, we, too, must transition into who God predestined us to be, and Peter helps us to understand a few things in his epistles. Focusing on his first epistle, Peter lets us know the value of the trials of faith and how grace brought us into the revelation of Christ. In chapter 2, he refers to believers as lively stones, chosen, royal, and peculiar. In chapter 4, Peter admonishes us to minister according to the ability God has given, to glorify God in suffering for Christ's sake. And in chapter 5, he encourages us to cast our cares upon the Lord— because He does care for us.

As you and I walk this path, we are in a continual cycle of discipleship, transitioning from one stage in Christ to the next. As you think about Peter and look at the lives of other prominent men and women of God, embrace the reality that we, too, are graced to become who God wants and purposed us to be. As we grow in Him and in the grace given us, we must show grace to others, as they, too, go through their developmental stages to become who God has called them to be. Remember, we, as believers, are graced to become more in Christ our Lord.

Jesus

Jon Featherstone

"And she shall bring forth a son, and thou shalt call his name Jesus: for he shall save his people from their sins." Matthew 1:21

O
ne encounter with Jesus and your life will never be the same again. In one moment, one of the most antagonistic persecutors of the Christian faith is transformed into one of the most zealous advocates of the Christian faith. How? Through one encounter with the living God. Not through a course, not through an intellectual argument, not through the power of persuasion, but one encounter with God. Christianity is more than a theory, more than an ideology, more than an argument or a debate. Christianity is about a real and living God encountering a broken and lost mankind. One encounter with God and the hardest man, the most unbelieving woman, can be transformed.

"Then Saul, still breathing threats and murder against the disciples of the Lord, went to the high priest and asked letters from him to the synagogues of Damascus, so that if he found any who were of the Way, whether men or women, he might bring them bound to Jerusalem. As he journeyed he came near Damascus, and suddenly a light shone around him from heaven. Then he fell to the ground, and heard a voice saying to him, "Saul, Saul, why are you persecuting Me?" And he said, "Who are You, Lord?" Then the Lord said, "I am Jesus, whom you are persecuting. It is hard for you to kick against the goads." So he, trembling and *astonished, said, "Lord, what do You want me to do?" Then the Lord said to him, "Arise and go into the city, and you will be told what you must do." And the men who journeyed with him stood speechless, hearing a voice but seeing no one. Then Saul arose from the ground, and when his eyes were opened he saw no one. But they led him by the hand and brought him into Damascus. And he was three days without sight, and neither ate nor drank"* Acts 9:1-8.

The Bible is a book of encounters. Not just a book of teachings, but a book that inspires us to say if God can meet them, then God can meet with me. God wants to meet with you. He is the God who delights in breaking into our world and revealing the greatness of who He is. One encounter changed my life and one encounter can change yours.

I was raised in a good home. My parents were good, loving people and yet at the age of seventeen, I went off the rails. I moved to London to study to become a Nurse. The only problem was I ended up taking more drugs than I gave out. Cannabis led to Speed. Speed led to Ecstasy, LSD, and cocaine. Then one weekend, it all went horribly wrong. I was in a night club in a speedway stadium in Kings Lynn and I had taken a gram of speed and an ecstasy tablet. I was dancing to the music when all of a sudden, I had a massive pain in my chest and I don't know if it actually happened, or if I was hallucinating, but I came out of my body, saw myself, and got back in my body. It completely freaked me out. I spent the rest of the night sitting in the corner. I was convinced I had died. My head was a complete mess. I felt like I had gone crazy.

The next day, I remember sitting down for lunch with my parents. I couldn't eat anything, and I just stared into space. I remember my mum crying. She didn't know what had happened to her son. She just knew that the boy in front of her was no longer the child she had raised. I returned to London and depression engulfed me. I would hear voices telling me to kill myself. "You are already dead anyway. Jump out of the window, nothing will happen." I continued to smoke Cannabis and paranoia gripped me every single day. I was eighteen and I had destroyed my life. It was my rock bottom.

Maybe things feel *rock bottom* for you today? I want to tell you everything can change. You're not reading this book by chance but *one encounter with God, and everything can change.*

My parents put their foot down and demanded I return home. I found a new poison—alcohol. I stopped smoking Cannabis and I found if I drank alcohol, then I could silence the voices in my head. I could numb the pain. So, I would drink every single night but the depression remained. Then one day, I was watching the T.V. programme *Touched by an Angel.* You might not have seen it but it is about three people who go around helping others but secretly, they are angels on assignments. I was watching the T.V. programme and I was so depressed and I said, "God, if You're really out there, if You will turn my life around, then I will be an angel for You. I had no idea what I had just prayed.

Two weeks later, a new person started working at the call centre that I worked for. He sat in the desk next to me and had a big old Bible on his desk. I thought he was weird. That same week, we ended up on a work's night out. It was free alcohol all night, I thought I was in "Heaven". I ended up sitting next to this guy again and so I turned to him and said, "You're one of those Jehovah Witnesses, aren't you?" I thought this because of his big Bible. He said, "No, I am a Christian." I said, "Oh! I'm a Christian, too." He laughed and said, "No, you are not a Christian." I said, 'Yeah, I am. I go to church on Christmas and Easter" (I had been maybe once). He laughed again and said, "No, you are not a Christian; if you were a Christian, you would not be living the way you are living. In fact, you should leave and come to church with me on Sunday and I will show you what a Christian is." I stood up and left.

I stood outside the venue and I was thinking what am I doing outside here! I phoned my Dad and he came and picked me up. My Mum and Dad were incredible; even when I was at my worst, they continued to show me love and unconditional acceptance. I called my Dad and he drove to fetch me because he wanted to make sure I got home safe. I got in the car and he said, "What are you doing home this early? And you're sober! What is going on?" I laughed and said, "I don't know."

That Sunday, I went to Phil's church. He was the assistant pastor. When I walked in the door, I felt like I had come home. All through worship, tears flowed down my cheeks. This was what I had been looking for. You see, church is about more than singing songs in a building and a man speaking a message. There is One who dwells in the midst. God was there and His presence was my home. I accepted Jesus Christ into my life that day. I accepted that He died on the Cross in my place, so that I could be free. One moment in His presence. One encounter with God, and my life was never the same again.

Three days later, I went back to the church to help two dear old ladies pack boxes to send to orphans in Romania. They had asked for a volunteer and I was the muscles they needed! I lifted boxes and stacked them for the ladies but after a while, they stopped me and said, "Can we pray for you?" They began to pray 5 minutes, 10 minutes, 20 minutes, 25 minutes. For 30 minutes, they prayed for me. I was looking around thinking *what are they doing*? Hurry up, I have to go to work. But they kept on praying. Then, all of a sudden, my leg began to shake. I thought what on earth is that? And I began to sing in tongues. I began to sing in a language I had never heard of, and I didn't know.

I had never read in the Bible of Acts 2 and the Day of Pentecost. I had never heard of the Baptism in the Spirit. I had never heard anyone else speaking in tongues and here I was singing in tongues. The two old ladies stopped praying and went back to work and I was none the wiser. I left and walked to work and it was like my whole world had changed. The sky was different. The grass was different. The world had gone from black and white to high definition colour. I felt alive. I was full of joy. **One encounter with Jesus and my whole life had changed**!

Within weeks, I had stopped drinking, taking drugs, smoking, gambling, swearing, and so on. Without anyone beating me with a Bible, I had become a new creation. I was finding joy in prayer and the Word. Joy in a vibrant relationship with the risen Jesus Christ. *One encounter with God and everything had changed*. But God didn't stop with just me. Six months later, my little brother (aged 12) gave his life to the Lord. Six months after that, my Mum gave her life to the Lord. A week later, my Dad gave his life. The three of them were baptized at the same time. At their baptism, my sister gave her life to the Lord and it wasn't long before her husband followed her into the Kingdom of God. **One encounter with God and everything changed**!

We need to be careful with our courses and programs that we don't win people's heads and leave their hearts miles away from God. God does not want to be a theory; He wants you to experience Him. To walk with Him like Adam walked with Him in the Garden of Eden. In Christ, you are destined for a life of adventure with the Holy Ghost. The Bible is not a book of theories and arguments; it's a book about men and women who encountered God.

A man with an experience is never at the mercy of a man with an argument. If you argue someone into the Kingdom, they can be argued out of the Kingdom but if someone encounters God, everything changes. You will never persuade me that my wife isn't real. I met her this morning, she is a wonderful woman of God. I love her to bits. In the same way, you won't persuade me that Jesus Christ isn't real. I met with Him this morning. He is wonderful. I love Him to bits. People don't need more knowledge, they need to be placed into an environment where they can encounter God.

Adam encounters God in the Garden of Eden. Abraham encounters God and receives promises for his future. Moses encounters God through a burning bush; a cloud by night and a fire by day. Elijah encounters God through a still small voice. David encounters God and is declared a man after God's own heart. Daniel encounters God and receives a visitation from an angel after 21 days of prayer. Isaiah encounters God when he sees the Lord high and lifted up and the train of His robe filled the Temple. Peter encounters God on a mountain when Jesus was transfigured before him. Paul encounters God on a Damascus road and millions across the world, and throughout the generations, have encountered this God-man Jesus Christ and their worlds have been turned completely upside down.

What will your encounter with Jesus look like? I don't know. God has a unique personal experience for you. However, He has made promises to meet with you. On the Cross, Jesus died and the Bible says that the Temple curtain was ripped in two. God declared that through the Cross, through the shed blood of His Son, He had made the way for us to come into the Holy of Holies, the place where His presence dwells. God is no longer far away, but He is near to all who call on His name.

Jeremiah 29:13 says, *"You will seek me and find me when you seek me with all your heart."*

Hebrews 11:6 says, *"But without faith it is impossible to please and be satisfactory to Him. For whoever would come near to God must [necessarily] believe that God exists and that He is the rewarder of those who earnestly and diligently seek Him [out]."*

One Encounter and everything can change! Seek Him now. Pray and worship until you find Him. He wants to meet with you now!

Lot

Chancey Heyward

"And when the morning arose, then the angels hastened Lot, saying, Arise, take thy wife, and thy two daughters, which are here; lest thou be consumed in the iniquity of the city." Genesis 19:15

Lot was one who liked nice things, and had amassed great wealth since being with his Uncle Abram. His wealth had become so great that the Bible says, *"..so that the land could not support both of them dwelling together; for their possessions were so great..."* Genesis 13:6, ESV. Abram told Lot that there was enough land for them to separate as far as they wanted to, so both would have sufficient space for their livestock and possessions. After surveying the land, Lot chose the land of the Jordan Valley because of how it looked. Lot noticed that *"...the Jordan Valley was well watered every-where like the garden of the Lord...."* Genesis 13:10, ESV.

No matter what it looks like, we have to yet seek God, to confirm that it's the path He has provisioned and predestined for our lives. For we are to *"Seek ye first the kingdom of God and his righteousness, and all these things shall be added unto you"* Matthew 6:33, KJV. Had Lot done so, he could've saved his entire family. Lot's journey reminds me of the passage for us to *"...be in the world, but not of the world"* John 17:15. Now, one could look at Lot's story two different ways. Why would a believer want to live in a city like Sodom, which was known for their wickedness? Here's where it could be debated that, we are to *go into the hedges and highways compelling those to come to Jesus,* Luke 14:23, KJV.

The Bible isn't clear on if Lot was winning souls to Christ while living in Sodom, but it does lend us to believe that he had risen to a level of prominence in that he was sitting at the gate, as in the custom of the day, only prominent figures could do so. One of my initial thoughts about Lot is his poor judgement to move his family in the heart of such a wicked and evil city. Now, you not only put yourself in temptation's sight picture, but you subject your wife and children to it, as well. I'm sure you've heard the phrase that life is a series of lessons and/or seasons, but the key is to learn from them, so you don't have to repeat it.

We cannot make decisions for ourselves, or our families, based on what things look like. As we know, our God has the ability to see much further down the road than we can, so we must walk by faith and not by sight in all things, no matter what it looks like. If it looks bad, walk by faith; if it looks good, walk by faith even the more, because that's when it's even more likely to backfire on you. It almost makes you wonder, "Why was Lot even mentioned in the Bible?" It's almost nothing good in there about him. Well, here's my submission to you about Lot's significance in the Bible. We, as human beings, learn two ways: what to do, and what not to do. Lot was one example of what NOT to do. Just to give you an idea of how wicked Sodom was, Abram pleaded with the angel prior to them going to Sodom and Gomorrah, that if there were at least 10 people in the city who were righteous, they wouldn't destroy it. The barter actually started with fifty righteous, and Abram worked it all the down to just 10. Well, you know how the story goes, the angels destroyed Sodom and Gomorrah, as there weren't even 10 people in the city who were righteous.

Even after the angel told Lot that the city would be destroyed, he still procrastinated and tried to barter against the angel's instructions. The instruction was to flee to the hills, but Lot didn't think the hills would be sufficient, so he asked if they could flee to the nearest city to avoid destruction. I would love to believe that if I received a forewarning that my house was going to be destroyed, I need to get my family out immediately. I want to believe that I wouldn't ask any questions and just get my family out, as that would be the #1 priority. But if I'm being honest, I would probably ask if I can take a few things with me. I can easily see myself through the lens of Lot, as I was a procrastinator as well; and if I'm not careful, I still find myself struggling in that area from time to time. Thank God for the woman/wife that God has given me who keeps me on track, as procrastination tries to rear its ugly head. Lot's procrastination was so severe that even after he was told to take his family and leave, the next morning came and he still hadn't left. But was yet shown mercy and actually seized by the angels and led out of the city to safety. The word "seized," as mentioned in Genesis 19:16, meant that they were actually taken by the hand and led out of the city, because the Bible says, ... *"But he lingered"* Genesis 19:16, ESV.

"The effectual fervent prayer of a righteous man availeth much," James 5:16. Even in the midst of Lot's bargaining, instead of obedience, it was Abram that God remembered and yet spared his life. At the age of four months, I was taken in and reared by my birth mother's best friend and her husband. My mother was living the street life, and wasn't ready to give it up, so they took me in as their own. Back then, there was no paperwork, no adoption, no custody battles, or courts. Little did I know then that I was the manifestation of an answered prayer by the wife and woman who I came to know as *Ma*.

You see, they had a son of their own; an only child who was a star both on and off the court and the field. Lettered in basketball, football, and track who was a freshman at Florida Agricultural and Mechanical University (FAMU) majoring in Electrical Engineering. He was on his way back home to Polk County, FL one weekend and became the victim of a head on collision from a drunk driver, which landed him in a coma that he would never recover from. After about six months into this life changing event, my mother decided to pull the plug, and the brother I never got a chance to really know was gone forever. In the midst of all of this, my mother was going through a battle of her own. She had decided to give up her life in the world to follow Christ, which is right around the time she prayed and asked God to bless her with another son, whom she would promise to raise him "in the Lord," as they said back then. Here comes this lil ol' crying baby Chancey, who they had been babysitting off and on since he was born. She quickly realizes that I was the answer to the prayer she prayed, and she endeavored on the journey to raise me up in the way that I should go.

I have been in church from as early as I can remember, as it became my lifestyle. If we weren't physically IN church, it was on the satellite T.V. and back then, whatever channel the main T.V. was on, all other T.V.'s in the house mirrored that channel. I ate, slept, and breathed church, and definitely had a love/hate relationship with it. I loved the way I felt when the power of God would fall in the service or even as I watched some of the old patriarchs on television, but I hated that I couldn't attend dances, parties, and other events taking place "outside" of church in my neighborhood, because they were worldly! I knew from a young age that there was a strong call of God on my life, but I ran from it as best I could.

In high school, I was in ROTC, and in marching band, so I could get out of having to go to church on Friday nights. Because I was in the marching band, I was able to go to the football games on Friday nights, and see my girlfriend… which was a huge "No, No" in my house at the time, even though I was in high school. ROTC was my ticket to ditch our small town and go live a little. I signed up for delayed entry into the Army in my Junior year of high school, because I wanted nothing more than to leave and never have to be made to go to church again. After graduation, I was raising my hand for the US Army a week later. After my training, I was off to the far country of Germany and I was beyond excited, except to be leaving my longtime girlfriend. I set out on a course to do any and everything I thought my parents had been trying to keep me from. Like Lot, anything God was leading me to, I was looking to go the other direction. In the midst of my waywardness, I knew that my mother was praying for me, and I knew those prayers were also covering me, just as Abram's prayers covered Lot and his family even when he couldn't see the mercy that was being shown toward him.

I was truly "that guy," and had no idea how far from God I was. I can recall standing in a club one evening, hearing the voice of God say to me… "What are you doing here?" I had no desire or satisfaction in it anymore, but I wasn't ready to commit to God and walk away from doing things my own way and living my life on my own terms. Well, let me just say, God has a way of "encouraging" you to think twice about the direction your life is heading. I was on my way back to my base o'dark thirty, one morning after being promiscuous. I left the young lady's house around 2:30am, only to be flipped over in a ditch at 2:45am from falling asleep at the wheel. In the midst of that accident, I literally released the steering wheel and God had control of my vehicle as it was spinning on a two-lane highway with ditches on either side. As the vehicle was spinning, I heard God's voice audibly saying to me, "This is your last chance," repeatedly. As scary as that sounds, there was an unreasonable peace upon me, as I knew that I had a chance, even it was my last one.

I managed to climb out of my totaled vehicle up to the road, after the roof was crushed by the tree that stopped my decent down the ditch. It's only by God's grace that I didn't have on a seatbelt and was thrown to the passenger floor of the car, which actually saved my life. Oh it gets even better... as tractor trailer drivers were zooming by, an ambulance shows up as they are headed to another call, but just so happen to pass by me and noticed me standing on a two-lane back road with no shirt on and found that strange. They stopped, asked me how I got there and what was going on, as they couldn't see my vehicle at the bottom of the ravine off the road. After all of that, I had no injuries, broken bones, cuts, bruises, or any signs that I had been in that severe of an accident. They cleared me, called me a tow truck, and proceeded to their next call.

As traffic starts to build up, because the tow truck had the two-lanes blocked, he had to climb down the ravine to attach the tow hook to the vehicle in order to pull it up to the road. There were onlookers waiting for the vehicle to come up, so they could see if anyone, or who, was in the vehicle. They were all shocked to hear that it was me who was driving the car, and I'm standing right here beside them on the road. No one could believe I emerged from the wreck that was before them. If nobody else knew who and why I was standing there on that road, able to tell them it was me driving that totaled vehicle... I knew!

God saved my life! Just as Lot's life was saved from the destruction of Sodom and Gomorrah. He didn't want to leave, he procrastinated when told that it would be destroyed; he even bartered to go elsewhere, other than where the angel of the Lord instructed him to go and was still shown mercy. In the end, the very place the angel told him to go initially is where he ended up going, because he was afraid to live in Zoar due to way the inhabitants lived in Sodom. This time, he wasn't taking any chances, so he fled to the very hills he was originally instructed to go with his two daughters.

No matter what it looks like, know that God knows the beginning from the end and He has your best interest at heart. He promised to never leave or forsake us, so if you ever feel alone, check your compass to see if it's actually you who's strayed away from Him. I know my mother prayed for me, and it's her prayers that allowed me to come back home to God. Those prayers allowed me, just like the prodigal, to wake up in the midst of the pigpen and realize that I no longer had to live like this. For those who grew up like me, the world looks appetizing, inviting, tempting, and desirable, but don't be deceived, because it's only a distraction to pull you away from your God given purpose.

I am grateful for the journey that put me back on track and in alignment with my purpose and calling, because it helps me to realize that no matter the detour, obstacles, or setbacks, God can use it all, and it's what makes us so individually unique and impactful. I've said this many times before, I believe there are people in this life who are assigned to each of us, and are simply waiting on us to get into position, so their lives can be changed because of us. Your story matters, and God wants to use it to add to the Kingdom in His own way. You may not understand it all, but just be obedient. I'm sure Lot probably wondered why the instructions were to run and not look back. Why not look back? What could that hurt to just look and see? We may not always understand God's intentions, motives, or methods, but trust His leading.

Allow God to be your guide, the person of the Holy Spirit to lead you into all truth and always seek to please God above all.

The Apostle Paul

Jim Cutter

"Paul, an apostle, (not of men, neither by man, but by Jesus Christ, and God the Father, who raised him from the dead;)" Galatians 1:1

While on his way to Damascus to continue persecuting followers of the Way, Paul has a life-changing encounter with Jesus. During this powerful moment, Paul is knocked to the ground, loses His natural sight and in the form of an open vision, receives instructions from the Lord. Once Paul arrives in Damascus, the Spirit directs a disciple named Ananias to find him. Ananias lays hands on Paul to restore his sight and prophesy to Him, that he is a chosen vessel who will endure much suffering for the sake of the Lord's name.

"Now there was a disciple at Damascus named Ananias; and the Lord said to him in a vision, "Ananias." And he said, "Here I am, Lord." And the Lord said to him, "Get up and go to the street called Straight, and inquire at the house of Judas for a man from Tarsus named Saul, for he is praying, and he has seen in a vision a man named Ananias come in and lay his hands on him, so that he might regain his sight." Then Ananias answered, "Lord, I have heard from many about this man, how much harm he has done to Your saints in Jerusalem. And here he has authority from the chief priests to bind all who call on Your name." But the Lord said to him, "Go, for he is a chosen instrument of Mine, to bear My name before the Gentiles and kings and the sons of Israel; for I

will show him how much he must suffer for My name's sake" Acts 9:1016, NASB.

In the narrative above, we discover what I believe to be one of the most notable and yet under-celebrated truths regarding the life and ministry of Paul. From the very beginning of his conversion, he was told two facts: he was a chosen vessel and that he would suffer and endure much difficulty for the sake of the Gospel. The question that arises in my mind is this: What could Paul have been thinking after receiving such a profound word? Throughout much of the New Testament, it is clear Paul was well acquainted with suffering. At times, he seems to elevate suffering to such a degree that one might think he is advocating it as a normative practice, a practice that followers of Christ should embrace, not simply avoid. Though I don't believe Paul's intention was to encourage believers to run towards suffering, he does seem to advocate that there is a Kingdom-minded response and a grace given by Holy Spirit to empower believers to walk through and do hard things.

A HEALTHY THEOLOGY OF SUFFERING

Paul encourages us in 2 Corinthians 8-10, NLT: *"We are pressed on every side by troubles, but we are not crushed. We are perplexed, but not driven to despair. We are hunted down, but never abandoned by God. We get knocked down, but we are not destroyed. Through suffering, our bodies continue to share in the death of Jesus so that the life of Jesus may also be seen in our bodies."*

Paul profoundly and humbly draws our attention to his present suffering and the story of redemption. His imagery draws a clear parallel between the Cross and the Resurrection of Jesus and the deep suffering through which He was walking. Paul viewed hardship, difficulty, and suffering through the lens of eternity and as a continual reminder of the power presented to us through the Cross and Resurrection of Christ.

Nowhere do we find Paul ever getting angry at God or disappointed when things went differently than he had planned. Nor did he desire to deconstruct his faith. It would have been human for Paul to have these responses. Yet the presence of perseverance, strength, and even joy we see in Paul's exhortation calls us into deeper understanding of the grace of God and a healthy theology of suffering. It is not God's punishment but a divine invitation each disciple must answer as God works all things out for the good of those who love Him and are called according to His purpose, Romans 8:28-29. Paul has a higher perspective of his suffering and rightly recognizes it as the way his life is used to glorify Christ. Thousands of years later, it is this very tension of strength and endurance during deep suffering that continues to encourage modern disciples and advance the Gospel of Christ.

WHAT IS A WITNESS?

The invitation into suffering is seen in an unexpected place in Acts 1:8, NKJV. This truth is further illustrated when we look at the meaning of the word *witnesses*. *"But you will receive power when the Holy Spirit has come upon you; and you shall be My witnesses both in Jerusalem, and in all Judea and Samaria, and even to the remotest part of the earth."* This word in Greek is *martus,* a term that was used to denote those who bore witness to their faith, especially those who witnessed to the point of suffering, or dying, for their beliefs. It is from this Greek word that we derive the modern meaning and reference of the word *"martyr"*.

As modern day followers of Jesus, Acts 1:8 provides a faith-compass that guides us into a kind of witnessing that is imbued with power. Through the empowerment of the Spirit, we who believe have been given grace to testify of Christ through the things we suffer, even if it results in death.

Each of us living on this side of eternity understands that difficulty and suffering are all part of the human condition. Yet in his passionate pursuit to advance the Kingdom of God, Paul seems to thrive on the idea that suffering is the vehicle of declaring Christ throughout the entire known world. He makes it clear that suffering is not something to be avoided, but something to embrace. In 2 Timothy 2:1, 3 NLT, Paul tells his spiritual son Timothy to *"be strong through the grace that God gives you in Christ Jesus."* He exhorts Timothy to join in His suffering by encouraging him to *"endure hardship as a good soldier of Christ."*

THE GRACE OF AN APOSTOLIC LEADER

One of the qualities and qualifications of disciples of Jesus and especially apostolic leaders is the grace to endure suffering. What distinguishes Paul's apostolic leadership in his letters to the Church is his revelation of suffering. In various places and on numerous occasions, Paul draws our attention to what our response ought to be.

In 2 Timothy 2:10 NLT, Paul states: *"So I am willing to endure anything if it will bring salvation and eternal glory in Christ Jesus to those God has chosen."* The question I would propose to each of us is this: What are we willing to endure for the glory of Christ and for the advancement of Kingdom?

In the next two verses, Paul continues this theme, promising rewards for those who persevere in their faith, 2 Timothy 2:11-12: *"This is a trustworthy saying: If we die with him, we will also live with him. If we endure hardship, we will reign with him. If we deny him, he will deny us."*

The idea here is there is a reward that can only be attained by remaining faithful and steadfast in the midst of suffering. Life is not always fair, but God is always good. In summary, Paul calls us to live above the noise and adversity of our day while being relentless in faith and perseverance to trust God in all things.

A PERSONAL JOURNEY

I gave my life to Christ at 14 years old. Although I have made many mistakes along the way, I have endeavored to serve Him faithfully and trust Him through the complexities of life. In my formative years, I was raised in predominantly Pentecostal circles where suffering was not often discussed with much admiration. It was usually framed in one of two ways: either it was the work of the devil or it was an opportunity to give God glory when things finally straightened out. Generally, suffering was viewed through a lens similar to Job's friends: "What have you done wrong that God has forsaken, or is punishing, you?" To say the least, we did not have a healthy theology of suffering.

THE SEASON EVERYTHING CHANGED

In 2013, my wife and I, along with our four children and my sister and brother-in-law, felt led by the Lord to plant a church in our city. At the time, we were part of Regency Church in Whittier, California, where we had served with our Senior Leaders for over 20 years. We met with our spiritual parents to share our vision and seek their blessing. After a year and a half of preparation, we launched the new church on January 25, 2015.

One year into our church plant, I met with my spiritual parents, Dr. Jason and Dr. Cathy Guerrero. These meetings were always welcomed, but this one was different. Jason had been diagnosed with cancer. Despite the shock and the feeling of helplessness, I trusted in God's goodness and healing power to bring Jason through.

For the next three years, Jason fought courageously and our church family stood firm in prayer and faith. Yet on February 27, 2019, much to my disappointment, Jason passed away. His transition into eternity left me heartbroken and full of questions: "God, what are You doing? Why is this happening? This isn't how it was supposed to go." Over the next four years, we walked through a web of difficulty and challenging circumstances, too many to share. Yet each step of the way, God provided us grace, wisdom, and strength. In the life of a believer, suffering is rarely, if ever, the result of sin; it is simply part of being human.

MY REVELATION OF JESUS

As I reflect on the last eight years of my journey with Christ, I realize that I have come to know Him in ways I could never have discovered without experiencing suffering. Do I wish it could have been different? Of course. Yet, I have come to trust Him in all things. He is the Sovereign One, and I hold firmly to the conviction that God is good even when I can't see it. I joyfully serve at the pleasure of the King. Like Paul in his epistle to the Corinthian church, I recognize that I have been bought with a price and I am not my own. For me, to live is Christ and to die is gain.

There is something about the crucible of suffering, or the crushing of Gethsemane, that produces oil and fragrance we would never know apart from pain. May each of us be reminded of this, as stated by Paul, the Apostle of Suffering, in 2 Corinthians 12:9, NKJV: *"My grace is sufficient for you, for My strength is made perfect in weakness."*

My prayer for us all today is that our lives reflect Christ in such a way that even in our suffering, we become an expression of worship so that others may be strengthened and Christ be exalted.

Boaz

Arthur McFarlane, III

"And Naomi had a kinsman of her husband's, a mighty man of wealth, of the family of Elimelech; and his name was Boaz." Ruth 2:1

Boaz sees it all. Everything under Boaz was seen by Boaz, from the young men, to the young women, to his harvest. Boaz was a man of strength, integrity, and honor. He was a pillar in his family, a provider and a protector of that which was entrusted into his hands by God. And he was revealed as a redeemer according to Scripture. We are introduced to Boaz in the Book of Ruth. The backstory begins with Naomi's husband dying, as well as her two sons. Their wives followed Naomi to serve her as their mother in law. Naomi urged them both to return to their father's house, and that she would travel to her late husband's family's settlement. The one sister, Orpah, chose to return to her family, while Ruth made the decision that Naomi's family was now her family.

"Then Boaz said to his servant who was in charge of the reapers, "Whose young woman is this?" So the servant who was in charge of the reapers answered and said, "It is the young Moabite woman who came back with Naomi from the country of Moab. And she said, 'Please let me glean and gather after the reapers among the sheaves.' So she came and has continued from morning until now, though she rested a little in the house" Ruth 2:5-7

Boaz was intrigued by this young woman who chose to leave her family to be joined to his by way of Naomi, his relative's widow. He immediately made provision for Ruth and commanded her not to go another field to glean, but to remain in his care and that he would provide for her every need. The men were told not to touch her. Boaz gave freely of his estate to Ruth, a foreigner in the eyes of those on the outside, but to him, one that was grafted into his family tree by way of humility and honor. When Boaz notices one that needs help, he gives of himself and commanded those under him to give as well, even a little extra.

"Then Boaz said to Ruth, "You will listen, my daughter, will you not? Do not go to glean in another field, nor go from here, but stay close by my young women. Let your eyes be on the field which they reap, and go after them. Have I not commanded the young men not to touch you? And when you are thirsty, go to the vessels and drink from what the young men have drawn." So she fell on her face, bowed down to the ground, and said to him, "Why have I found favor in your eyes, that you should take notice of me, since I am a foreigner?" And Boaz answered and said to her, "It has been fully reported to me, all that you have done for your mother-in-law since the death of your husband, and how you have left your father and your mother and the land of your birth, and have come to a people whom you did not know before. The Lord repay your work, and a full reward be given you by the Lord God of Israel, under whose wings you have come for refuge" Ruth 2:8-12

Boaz was a man to be respected, not by force but through honor. His life exemplified a true man in every sense of the word. To ask me about the condition of *the modern man*, I would say that the knee jerk response I would have is Exhausted. It may just be me, I could be a man that's purely exhausted. I could also be one of many men who are simply tired, confused, and unsure of the social climate and cues that exist in the modern world.

What is it to be a man in this world but not *of this world*. What does it mean to be "manly"? With words like *alpha man* and *high value man* flowing through the streams of social media, viral personalities are constantly taking sides that have proven to be antiquated, out of touch, and stretching towards the extreme. But so many people have drunk from the well of opinions not so much based on fact, but on their own feelings and perceptions.

Most of the time those feelings are rooted in loneliness, fear, and depression. Probably guilt, anger, and shame, as well. At least this was the case for me. I was pulling myself from the abyss that was a public and humiliating divorce. And in the depths, I looked for something to pull me out of the darkness and into the light. I was desperate for validation and encouragement to show me that I was worthy. Worthy of love. Worthy of acceptance. Worthy of connection. Worthy to someone, and belonging to something. Yet as so many turned to podcasts, personalities, and performances, I turned to something greater. The Holy Word—the ultimate text for all things.

"And you will seek Me and find Me, when you search for Me with all your heart" Jeremiah 29:13

When you are lost, confused, in a pool of misery, the Bible contains content that will bring light, clarity, and encouragement to every situation that you find yourself in. And I was in a situation of surviving ideation of suicide, self-doubt, and mental and spiritual masochism that rivaled a Shakespearean lead character. *To be or not to be* was a daily question and thankfully, my God, through His Word, had answers. I found some of those answers to my identity, my self-esteem, and my worthiness in the Book of Ruth where I felt I met for the first time, Boaz.

Now, we have all heard of Boaz. He is the main topic of conferences, sermons, and even songs. I would know, as I have participated in many of those conferences; I've heard those sermons and I've sang those songs. Boaz has been a dream of many women and an almost mythological hero for most men. But in my darkest hour, when I needed answers about my identity as a man, a *modern man,* I saw Boaz as the standard.

To share my story along with my time with Boaz would make this devotional into a full book and possibly, it may come to pass. But for now, I'd like to share some indelible characteristics of Boaz that I began to emulate; or at least aspire to as I walked the slow, arduous journey out of the valley of mental unwellness onto a path towards my calling.

Boaz believed and walked in absolute *redemption*. He did not give a second thought to redeem his kinsman's widow, as this was custom and tradition. But more importantly, it was seen as legacy and generational familial security. Boaz is bold in his integrity and accountability. Even when there is a *shade of gray*, Boaz steers the ship down the narrow path that ultimately redeems all in his sphere of influence. This man is one to not only emulate, but also to fear. Not fear in the sense of being afraid of or intimidated by, but in respect and reverence due to his faithfulness and commitment not only to his family, but also to his God. He placed a high value on redemption. Our Father sent the ultimate Redeemer to free us from this life of sin. Boaz was a type and shadow of our Lord, Jesus Christ.

The Bible declared Boaz as *worthy* to be the redeemer for Ruth as he was a close relative, he was well-known, he owned land, and he oversaw a harvest. His influence and status in his community paved the way for his voice to not only be heard, but to be obeyed by his family and neighbors. He welcomed Ruth, a foreigner, into his family and commanded the others to treat her as one of their own. Such is the character of our Kinsman Redeemer, Jesus Christ, our Lord and Savior. He welcomes us into the family of God, not imputing our sins against us and grants to us the right to be heirs of His Kingdom.

"There was a relative of Naomi's husband, a man of great wealth, of the family of Elimelech. His name was Boaz. So Ruth the Moabitess said to Naomi, "Please let me go to the field, and glean heads of grain after him in whose sight I may find favor" Ruth 2:1-2

Boaz was also *kind* and greeted everyone he crossed paths with, with a *blessing*. He enthusiastically made himself available to those that gleaned in his fields. He did not treat them as slaves, or even as workers; he saw the value in each and every person that God had given unto his care and treated them with dignity and honor. Due to his honorable leadership, this kindness and blessing was returned unto him a hundred fold.

"Then he said, "Blessed are you of the Lord, my daughter! For you have shown more kindness at the end than at the beginning, in that you did not go after young men, whether poor or rich. And now, my daughter, do not fear. I will do for you all that you request, for all the people of my town know that you are a virtuous woman" Ruth 3:10-11

This has always been my heart as a man, sometimes to my own detriment. I have given of myself completely to those that I loved, respected, and trusted to hold my heart and my hand with honesty and integrity. Unfortunately, in some cases, I was left shattered in a million pieces by betrayal and embarrassment. But praise be to God, through His Word, He has brought great healing and deliverance to my life. I don't want to be the man that seeks revenge or the downfall of those that have sought to destroy my life; I want to be a man like Boaz who walked in kindness and was respected as a great leader to those around him. We do not have to become like those have wronged us. May we rise above the hurt, pain, disappointment, and betrayal to emerge as holy, men of God.

Another character trait of Boaz that I seek to walk in is *grace*. Grace is the ability to offer to others what may not be deserved, but what is right in the eyes of God. None of us deserve salvation. The Bible says that we are all sinners and that we have all fallen short of His glory. Even in my darkest days, there were times where I did not recognize myself at all. I had lost much of who I was due to such a public betrayal, especially being it extended from the hands of a trusted spiritual leader. It took me years to come to some sort of normalcy of healing. Though we may not want to hear it, God's Word is truth and He tells us that if we cannot forgive the sins of our brothers and sisters, then He will not forgive us of ours. It takes grace to forgive and it took grace for Boaz to extend his hand to a woman that was a foreigner, one that was not of his own lineage.

"For there is no difference; for all have sinned and fall short of the glory of God, being justified freely by His grace through the redemption that is in Christ Jesus," Romans 3:22b-24.

My story may not be yours, but as men, we all have a lot that we face in this evil and wicked world. The enemy seeks to destroy the very essence of who we are as sons of God, sons of purpose, in the Earth. He will direct every dart and wield every weapon in his arsenal toward us to move us out of our position in Christ. He seeks to corrupt and pervert the goodness within us which was created in us from the Beginning. He desires to kill, to steal, and to destroy every good and perfect gift that God places in our lives, especially and most importantly, our marriages and our families, which is the foundation of His image in the Earth. May we stand and fight with all that is within us not only for our place and position in Christ as godly and holy men, but also for one another. May we hold one another accountable to the same holy standards that we set for ourselves.

Boaz didn't simply *talk the talk*; he *walked the walk*. May we not only be men of our word, but men of His Word. May we look to the example of Boaz's life, so we can lead our families in the path of right-eousness and holiness. That we may be the salt and the light in the Earth. That we may be that city set upon the hill that the world can see and run to it, to Him.

I am encouraged to go on and fulfill the call of God in my life, and I pray that you are, as well. He redeemed Ruth. He redeemed me. And He will redeem you, too. Just because things may have been declared "dead" in your life does not mean that God is finished with you. Some things have to die in your life in order for you to be introduced to new life in Him. There is hope in Christ. Christ in us, the Hope of Glory.

Haggai

Ronnie F. Brown

"Then spake Haggai the Lord's messenger in the Lord's message unto the people, saying, I am with you, saith the Lord." Haggai 1:13

I am writing about the prophet Haggai. He was one of the twelve *minor* prophets that was not well liked by the people of his day because he was "set aside by God". Growing up, I felt *minor* because we did not have what other kids in the neighborhood had. I used to say, "I wish I was normal like the other kids." We would have luncheons at school, but I could not participate because I could not afford two dollars. Therefore, low self-esteem set in. The other kids would laugh because they knew during these special days my mom would take me out of school, because we could not afford it.

I never blamed God for our shortcomings. At an early age, I knew it was something that needed to be corrected within me. It took a while to correct, because I did not know how and did not have a male figure in my life to teach me. I began to try to hang out with individuals who were popular. I walked in the room one day to find out I was the topic of the discussion in a negative way. This was a vicious cycle in my life during my childhood.

My life began to turn around in high school because I found out I was not the only one dealing with low self-esteem. When I turned my life over to Christ, things began to change. I did not notice the change immediately, as I did not know what to look for; it seemed like it was not happening fast enough. I began to realize that the reason I was talked about and laughed at was because I was, indeed, "set aside by God". He did not want me to get too comfortable with people.

After graduating high school, I joined the Navy. God began to take me around the world, physically, to show me that there are people far worse off than me. These experiences allowed me to mature at a faster pace while traveling around the world. I did not realize, at the time, that He was preparing to take me around the world, spiritually. It took years to rid myself of the spirit of low self-esteem. From time to time, the devil tries to bring it back up, but I am grateful that I am in a more mature place spiritually.

The Bible is not clear in revealing if Haggai had low self-esteem, but it is evident that he was deeply concerned about the people not receiving his prophecies about rebuilding the Temple after they had escaped from seventy years of captivity in Babylon/Persia.

"In the second year of King Darius, in the sixth month, on the first day of the month, the word of the Lord came by Haggai the prophet to Zerubbabel the son of Shealtiel, governor of Judah, and to Joshua the son of Jehozadak, the high priest, saying, "Thus speaks the Lord of hosts, saying: 'This people says, "The time has not come, the time that the Lord's house should be built." Then the word of the Lord came by Haggai the prophet, saying, "Is it time for you yourselves to dwell in your paneled houses, and this temple to lie in ruins?"

"Now therefore, thus says the Lord of hosts: "Consider your ways!"

"You have sown much, and bring in little; You eat, but do not have enough; You drink, but you are not filled with drink; You clothe your-selves, but no one is warm; And he who earns wages, Earns wages to put into a bag with holes."

"Thus says the Lord of hosts: "Consider your ways!" Haggai 1:1-7.

I was not popular with the guys at school; Haggai was not popular with the people of his day because his prophecies were not popular. Haggai had to prophesy to the people that their priorities were not in order. I am finally at a point in my life where I am not trying to become popular with the world. I am not trying to please anyone if they are not lined up with the Word of God.

"Do not love the world or the things in the world. If anyone loves the world, the love of the Father is not in him" 1 John 2:15.

Just remember, if you are dealing with low self-esteem, or whatever it is that you may be personally experiencing, refuse to give up and don't blame God. You do not fit in with the world because you have been "set aside by God". He is molding, shaping, and transforming you to do the work He has for you in this life.

I leave you with this!

"And we know that all things work together for good to those who love God, to those who are the called according to His purpose" Romans 8:28.

Gideon

Eric Brown

"Now Gideon perceived that He was the Angel of the Lord. So Gideon said,
"Alas, O Lord God! For I have seen the Angel of the Lord face to face."
Judges 6:22

Twelve years ago, my youngest daughter was hit by a SUV while helping on our church's bus route. Doctors did not expect her to live; however, God had other plans. Jehovah Rapha spared her life and miraculously healed her. She had to relearn how to walk, talk, eat, drink, and many other things we take for granted. Her testimony was shared on Facebook each day of her recovery and impacted so many lives. We received countless messages and letters telling us how what the Lord did through our daughter helped people, changed lives, and even brought revival to churches as they joined together to pray for her. She lives today, forever changed, living with a severe traumatic brain injury. After returning home from the hospital, my daughter would often ask why God allowed her to be hit by a car. I struggled to answer her, but usually told her that the Lord had a special plan and calling for her life. Looking back on the past twelve years, I still believe that the Lord has a calling on her life. Now, this is not your normal call from God. Usually, He does not cause someone He is calling to be hit by a car and almost die. My daughter's calling is indeed unusual.

Someone else in the Bible had an unusual calling. This was during a time of great apostasy in the nation of Israel. The Israelites found themselves in the midst of oppression, this time by the hand of the Midianites. Seven long years, they languished and suffered under the rule of this Gentile nation. Judges 6:6 says,

"And Israel was greatly impoverished because of the Midianites; and the children of Israel cried unto the LORD."

Then one day, Gideon was doing what he could to feed his family. The Midianites had stolen all of the food and crops in the land of Israel. Gideon threshed wheat by the winepress, to hide it from the Midianites, according to Judges 6:11. All of a sudden, the angel of the Lord appeared to him. Gideon did not immediately recognize him as an angel. The "man" says to Gideon:

"The LORD is with thee, thou mighty man of valor" Judges 6:12.

Now, this is a very interesting greeting! Imagine, you are out working in a wine press, trying to farm out some food for your family. You are afraid that the enemy may come at any time and try to steal what little you have. Yet, here is some person calling you a mighty man of valor. For those familiar with the account of Gideon, we know that the Lord God does indeed use him to deliver his people from the Midianites. What I want us to look at is his unique calling. It may be that God is calling you to do something for him. Or, you want to be used by the Lord, but do not hear His calling in your life. My prayer is that something about Gideon's calling will resonate with you and the Lord will use this to speak to and change your heart!

There are several things we know about Gideon's calling from God. The first thing is that <u>God calls a serving man</u>. In the first part of Judges 6:11, we find Gideon serving. He was threshing wheat in a winepress, to hide it from the Midianites. He was doing what he could, in the best way that he was able. He was not sitting idly by, hoping and praying for God to do something. It is rare that the Lord will call someone who is sitting around and doing nothing. You may go to church and sing worship songs. You may occasionally read your Bible and pray. What are you doing to serve the Lord where you are at? It may not be much. It may not be visible, in front of everyone; but there is something for you to do right where you are at. What are you doing to serve the Lord while waiting for His call?

Secondly, we see that God calls a hidden man. Gideon was hiding in a winepress. A winepress was usually a brick-lined hole in the ground where grapes would be poured into. In the middle was a deeper hole where the juice would fill after being stomped. In the Bible, the winepress is a picture of God's wrath and judgment. Jesus Christ was crushed and His blood was poured out in the winepress of God's wrath, while on the Cross of Calvary. Are you hidden in Christ? Do you spend more than a few measly minutes with Him throughout the day? Do you have full fellowship with Him, not just religious duties and obligations?

"That which we have seen and heard declare we unto you, that ye also may have fellowship with us: and truly our fellowship is with the Father, and with his Son Jesus Christ" 1 John 1:3.

God the Father and Jesus Christ the Son both desire to have sincere and meaningful fellowship with you!

The third thing we notice in verse 12 about Gideon's calling is that God calls a heroic man. God sees us differently than we see ourselves. The angel refers to Gideon as a "mighty man of valour." We will soon see that Gideon did not agree with this description. Yet, the Lord saw him as such. The Lord does not look on the outer appearance but on the heart. He sees what we cannot. Gideon did not see himself as a hero, yet the Lord saw differently. Maybe you do not think you can do anything for God. You do not have the qualifications you might think are needed. The Lord sees in you what you cannot. Trust Him to use you as He sees and knows you.

Next, in verse 13, we discover that God calls a struggling man. Gideon wondered what happened to the power of God. He had not experienced the miracles and wonders that he had heard about. Gideon felt like God had forsaken them. He struggled with his faith. How could he expect God to miraculously deliver his people when that was not something he had experienced before? We live in a day, and nation, where it seems God's power has fallen short. We do not see the miracles and healings we've heard about previously. Where are the revivals of years gone by? God's hand is not shortened so that it cannot save. He is the same yesterday, today, and forever! His power has not lessened! Perhaps He is waiting for you to answer His call.

In Gideon's call, we also see that <u>God calls a sent man</u>.

"And the LORD looked upon him, and said, Go in this thy might, and thou shalt save Israel from the hand of the Midianites: have not I sent thee?" Judges 6:14.

Know this, dear friend: if God calls you, He will send you. If God sends you, you have nothing to fear. He promised in Matthew 28:20 that He will be with us always, even unto the end of the world. He promises to never leave us nor forsake us, Hebrews 13:5-6. God will not just send you, He will go with you to accomplish His purpose in your life.

<u>God calls a humble man</u>. According to Gideon in Judges 6:15, he is part of a poor family and he is the least in his father's house. I do not believe Gideon is making excuses; this is something he truly believes. If you want to be used of God, remain humble. *"Pride goes before destruction, and a haughty spirit before a fall,"* Proverbs 16:18. God resisteth the proud. No matter what the Lord may be calling you to do, stay humble in His sight.

"And the LORD said unto him, Surely I will be with thee, and thou shalt smite the Midianites as one man" Judges 6:16.

Notice what the Lord told Gideon, "Surely I will be with thee." <u>God calls a sufficient man</u>. Not sufficient in ourselves, but as 2 Corinthians 3:5 tells us:

"Not that we are sufficient of ourselves to think any thing as of ourselves; but our sufficiency is of God;"

We are sufficient when we yield and surrender to the Lord in our lives. God will be with us and help us to do all that He is calling us to do.

In verse 17, we understand that <u>God calls a seeking man</u>. Gideon's faith wasn't perfect; yet he was seeking God's will. He asks the angel for a sign. We find later on, in verses 36-40, that Gideon asks another sign from God. We often think that asking for a sign is wrong. Yes, Jesus did say that an evil and adulterous generation seeketh after a sign. Yet, we find throughout the Bible where those God called ask for a sign regarding one thing or another. God never scorns a sincere heart that is seeking to believe. Perhaps your faith is not what you think it should be. Just continue seeking the Lord and His will in your life, and God will lead you in a plain path!

Lastly, we realize from the calling of Gideon that <u>God does not call a perfect man.</u> In verse 22-23, after the miracle the angel performs, Gideon realizes that he has come face to face with the angel of God.

"And when Gideon perceived that he was an angel of the LORD, Gideon said, Alas, O Lord GOD! for because I have seen an angel of the LORD face to face. And the LORD said unto him, Peace be unto thee; fear not: thou shalt not die" Judges 6:22-23

The Lord assures Gideon, declaring peace unto him and telling him not to fear. Today, the Lord is saying the same thing to you. We are all undeserving of God's calling and His presence in our lives. God doesn't call the worthy, He calls only the unworthy. He will equip and prepare us for the work that He has for each of us. In the following verses, God tells Gideon to go destroy the altar and grove of Baal that his father had set up. The calling of God will often require us to destroy the idols and altars we have set up in our lives. There can be nothing that comes before the Lord, if we are to do His will.

It was not until Gideon obeyed the Lord in tearing down his father's idols and altar, that the Lord God poured out His Holy Spirit upon Gideon, Judges 6:34. If you are waiting for God to fill you with the Holy Spirit before responding to His call, there may need to be a first step of obedience in your life. Gideon was afraid to do what God commanded him, so he did it at night while the others slept. However, he still obeyed the Lord. What is it that God is wanting you to do? Take that first step of obedience by faith, and God may, in turn, fill you with the Holy Spirit to do everything He is calling you to do.

If you are a born again believer, then I know God has a calling for your life. He will likely not send an angel to tell you, or allow something horrible to happen to you. Just know He is leading and guiding you and desires you to seek Him first, above all else. If you are unsure of what His calling is, just determine to seek Him with all your heart!

"And ye shall seek me, and find me, when ye shall search for me with all your heart" Jeremiah 29:13.

Paul

Daniel Jarvis

"Now the Lord spoke to Paul in the night by a vision, "Do not be afraid, but speak, and do not keep silent;" Acts 18:9

S o, where do I start? I suppose the beginning is a good place. Well, my name is Daniel. I was brought up in a Christian household, my Dad was an anointed Bible teacher and moved in the prophetic, and my Mom was involved in leading children's work and was a real prayer warrior! Reflecting back on my childhood, I can genuinely say I'm blessed by the start I had in life. We weren't well off, but we got by; there was always something in the fridge, we had a roof over our heads and shoes on our feet. There wasn't lots of spare money going for luxuries, but we were happy. I'm struck by how God paved the way for what lay ahead for me. God was at work even in the small things. Money was tight, yet like any other kid, I wanted things; one such thing was a trip to the movies. But Dad didn't have the money; instead, he proposed we pray for a solution. Miraculously, an anonymous envelope was pushed through the door later that day; it was the money we needed for the cinema. There are many more instances like this, all building in me a foundation of FAITH in Jesus.

Fast forward a few years, I'm ready to leave high school and deciding if I should go on to college, then university? I'm a bit of a geek, I've got good grades, and I enjoy learning, but as the oldest of the four of us kids, I needed my own space and like I said, money was always tight for us as a family. I didn't want to be a burden on Mom and Dad, so I decided to go get a job as an apprentice in an engineering firm. It was during this time that I met Marie; she visited the church I was attending. We sparked up a friendship, but I just knew she was the one for me, so I wore her down with roses and my charm. At 18 years old I got married, we bought a house, and started a life together. Wow, was that a shock to the system! Learning to live with someone, the stresses of running a house, and paying the bills. It was a real struggle at times. Throw into the mix something Marie had told me early on in our relationship... she couldn't have children... something we both wanted, and the fact that she was struggling with this far more than I had imagined, caused those early years of marriage to resemble a battle ground, at times.

My initial response to what Marie had told me had been, I found out the hard way, a little naive, "Don't worry about that, my God can do the impossible!" Let me just say now, HE CAN and DOES do the impossible, but that doesn't always happen when we expect it, or even how we expect it. Imagine what Peter, James, John, and the disciples in and around Jerusalem must have been feeling, as a man called Paul, a Pharisee, went about persecuting them?

"... I not only locked up many of the saints in prison ...but when they were to be put to death I cast my vote against them..." Acts 26:10.

I think they must have been asking God to deal with this guy, to sort him out. We don't know what they might have asked, but I have a feeling they weren't expecting God to answer in the way He did. In fact, we see the surprise at how God dealt with Paul, how He met the need of the disciples, but in His own way at a time He determined in Acts 9:26,

"...And when he had come to Jerusalem, he attempted to join the disciples. And they were all afraid of him, for they did not believe that he was a disciple..."

As we read on from here, we see that the disciples eventually caught up with God's plan. Paul was accepted into the family. But from the above, you can see they weren't expecting that answer; if they were, they wouldn't have been afraid. Maybe they had asked for a little less grace for Paul, possibly an Ananias and Sapphira ending? Don't forget, this was the man who had thrown their friends in prison, and had watched on and even cheered as they had been stoned. When it came to the death penalty, Paul was there casting his vote for it.

What might the Church have looked like if God had listened to the solutions put forward by His disciples? Would it have grown in the way it did? Would the Gentiles have had a voice in the early church like they had through Paul? God answered knowing the bigger picture, knowing that His solution would be the best solution, not just for Paul, but also for those frightened disciples, for His church, and even for us. I sit here typing as a Gentile believer and follower of Jesus, because Paul was spared, saved, and sent out to reach me, to reach us… Maybe, just maybe, God knows what He is doing when He answers prayers in His own way and timing… Just a thought…

Paul himself, when he asked God to deal with a 'thorn' in his side, having been on the mission field for a while, having seen God do some miraculous things, his faith in a good place, built up by the successes he was enjoying with God as he preached the good news of Jesus, asks God not just once, but three times to get rid of this thorn, and God answers him in a way I am sure he never expected. Read 2 Corinthians 12:8-9,

"… Three times I pleaded with the Lord about this, that it should leave me. But he said to me, "My grace is sufficient for you, for my power is made perfect in weakness."

God doesn't walk to the beat of our drum and sometimes, that can be really difficult to get our heads around. How many times do we tell God in our prayers how we expect, or want, that prayer to be answered, then we struggle when we don't hear or see what we want, or expect. Paul understood this struggle… the number of times he must have spoken to God and asked Him to heal someone, to provide, to cause a person to really get his message and turn to Jesus. We don't see those conversations with God in the Bible, but we see the result of some of them; we see how Paul is equipped for the next step, for the ministry that God has called him into. This equipping can only have come from a "No," "Not like that," or a "Not yet" from God.

"...Not that I am speaking of being in need, for I have learned in whatever situation I am to be content. I know how to be brought low, and I know how to abound. In any and every circumstance, I have learned the secret of facing plenty and hunger, abundance and need. I can do all things through him who strengthens me..." Philippians 4:11-13.

One of Paul's strengths is that he had his trust and faith firmly planted in Jesus, regardless of how Jesus answered his prayers. Paul was a man that was single minded, Jesus all the way. Having a faith like that is something I pray for, to be able to see and hear Jesus at work through Holy Spirit in every circumstance. Whether it is playing out the way I expected or not, to have that assurance that God has got this. I'd like to say I've got this lesson learnt, that I am totally at peace with handing my needs and desires over to God, being surrendered to however He sees fit to answer, but I'm still a work in progress...

My early years of marriage were a real training ground in this area. Like I said, Marie couldn't have children, and my naïve, and slightly immature, response was that blasé, "My God can do the impossible!" But for some years, He just didn't. I remember being frustrated, and not just a little discouraged, by the fact that our prayers for children had not been answered. We were a part of church life, going strong with God, and we had faith; why wasn't God answering us? Actually, I think God was answering us, we just weren't hearing. With hindsight, I can almost hear God's answer to those prayers,

"...My grace is sufficient for you, for my power is made perfect in weakness..."

But as a young couple, desperate for children, all we could hear at that time was silence. So, we tried to find an answer somewhere else; for us, it was the doctors. We had appointments and we pushed the doctors to try and help us... Eventually, they said yes. I don't know if you've ever done this, but we thanked God for opening that door. I see now that we were trying to chalk this up to God, because we needed to validate this path forward as God's *yes* to our prayers, to somehow show that

God was in agreement with us. It was backwards thinking, God agreeing with us? No, it should be us agreeing with God!

The next few years, however, would be some of the hardest of our lives, fertility treatments that ended in miscarriage after miscarriage, depression, our marriage becoming a rollercoaster ride of emotions, and a separation... a time of real pain. There was a particular moment during this whole saga where having been pregnant for some weeks, for the very first time, we had been sent back to the fertility hospital only to be told that we had lost the little one. I broke down in our bedroom, as I slid down the wall to the floor. I was just saying, "Why? Why God?" I said it over and over again. I can't remember the timeline exactly, it would have been some years later, but I sat in our bedroom again asking God, "Why?" But this time, not in an accusing way, not with a tone of blame, as if God had anything to be blamed for, but genuinely asking God, "Why? What happened? What went wrong?"

I remember having that feeling, that sense, of God speaking to me, it wasn't an audible voice like we hear about in Paul's encounter on the road to Damascus, but it was clear, gentle but firm, a voice speaking to me from somewhere inside, a bit like a thought that wasn't mine... "That was never how I was going to answer you. You rushed ahead and did it your own way." There was a feeling and tone in what I heard that felt warm, not condemning, but as if the person speaking, Holy Spirit, had been through that pain with us, had cried our tears, had felt everything we had felt, and right now, was simply answering my question *Why?* with the truth, but soaked in so much love and grace. It was at this point I started to get it; I started on that path of trusting God, truly trusting God, surrendering to Him no matter how He answered... That lesson that Paul got, to be content, I was starting to understand...

I'm not sure why you are reading this collection of devotionals, I don't know what you're going through right now, I don't know what you're praying for, but I do know that God answers, that even now as you read, He is answering. I also know that you are not alone if you've prayed prayers that plan out for God how and when to answer you, but let me encourage you to lay down your solutions, to trust God, He sees the bigger picture, He knows our needs, and He never gets it wrong. I started to learn a big lesson that day, we had rushed into answering our own prayers in our own way and it had been disastrous, and caused more years of hurt than you can imagine. We had to learn to trust in Him, to be *content* in whatever His answer was, and whenever He determined to answer. I'm fast forwarding through so much just to encourage you that when you submit to God, to His answers to your prayers, to His timing, you will see Him transform your life. Paul had to do just that, and look at who he became.

For us, we got to a place where we said to the doctors, *we need to step out of this process, this isn't God's answer for us*. They thought we were crazy, but we were ready to accept and surrender to God's answer, *Yes, or No*; whatever He chose, we had faith that He knew best.

"… for I have learned in whatever situation I am to be content. I know how to be brought low, and I know how to abound. In any and every circumstance, I have learned the secret of facing plenty and hunger, abundance and need. I can do all things through him who strengthens me…" Philippians 4:11-13.

Myself and Marie are stronger than ever. Years after coming off the fertility treatment, God blessed us with not one, but two beautiful daughters, Faith and Anaya-Grace, born without fertility treatment, complete and utter miracles. A story for another time maybe…

The Prophet Elijah

Mike Higley

"And it came to pass, at the time of the offering of the evening sacrifice, that Elijah the prophet came near and said, "Lord God of Abraham, Isaac, and Israel, let it be known this day that You are God in Israel and I am Your servant, and that I have done all these things at Your word."
1 Kings 18:36

Allow me to set the stage. Elijah, one of the greatest prophets of God in the Old Testament, had just challenged Jezebel's army of prophets to a showdown at Mount Carmel. Had he failed, Elijah would have been killed on the spot. But, by God's ability, Elijah was able to say "I told you so" to the 450 fake prophets and turn the table on Jezebel. Elijah's calling was to prove to the world that God is real and he did. But, as soon as Jezebel found out that Elijah had destroyed all of her prophets, she wanted payback. Not just a fine. She wanted him dead.

"When Elijah realized the seriousness of the threat, it scared him and he ran to hide" 1 Kings 19:3.

How soon we forget what God has done for us at the first sign of trouble. Elijah started backpedaling as soon as he sensed that things got uncomfortable. His calling became the very reason he was threatened.

In the early 1990s, I was regularly attending a local church in eastern Oklahoma and became close with the members there. My spiritual life was growing, and I began to sense a desire to help in different areas of the church. I filled in several times teaching a high school age Sunday School class and I soon realized that I connected easily to teen students. I was particularly drawn to the less privileged kids. They seemed to be looking for the most attention and were most receptive to God's Word. I got more involved by playing volleyball with them on Friday nights or going on trips with them.

I realized that not only was I drawn to them, but they were drawn to me as well. We just clicked. I began to feel that God was urging me to work with them. I didn't understand why He chose me, but I was both excited and scared about it. As I began to spend more time with the students in that church and mentor them, I began to feel drawn toward a feeling that God wanted me to do more. This was the first time in my life that I felt a "calling" from God. I struggled with the idea. Not only would I have to step up my game spiritually, but I also knew that other areas of my life would have to change. I worked at a manufacturing plant in Arkansas at the time, which was in the business of bottling alcoholic beverages. To me, it seemed to be a conflict of interest. I had a good paying job there and it did not seem very economical, or practical, to give it up.

One Monday morning, during my drive to work, I was praying as I drove. I do a big part of my talking with God while I drive. And, this particular day, I felt the urging of God to make a decision about whether I should give in to this or not.

"Alright," I told God. "I hear You loud and clear. I'll do whatever You want." At that very moment, I was so overwhelmed by the Holy Spirit that I began to cry. I felt so happy and peaceful, but it also scared me. I had just written a blank check to God. It was as if I were saying, "Here, God. You fill in the amount! I don't care what You want to do with me. Just fill it in!" That terrified me and I began to backpedal.

I'm not sure why, but I realized at that moment that I was not prepared to do what I told God I would do. But it was not my own preparation that determined my calling, but how God had been preparing me my whole life. I began to rationalize and think about all the things I might have to give up in order to commit to His ministry full time. I started thinking about the reason why I shouldn't do it. I wrestled with God. Every excuse I had for not moving forward with this, God had a reply. I worried about how much money I would have to give up. God sent a friend to tell me about a new verse he had read that told us not to worry about money in Matthew 6:25-28.

That Sunday, the sermon was about Elijah on the run from God right after God had used him to perform a miracle. Time after time, God kept asking Elijah *"what are you doing here?"*

Every reason I had for NOT giving my life to His calling, God had a reply. I began to run out of excuses and God was asking me the same thing… "Mike, what are you doing here? I want you there."

For almost a year, I did nothing. I guess I thought if I ignored it long enough, that God would move on to someone else. I was trying to put off a decision I had already made. I was stalling.

One beautiful Spring day, I was working in the back yard, burning dead leaves from the fall season. The grass was starting to turn green. This particular day, I had been thinking about my calling. We lived in a small, old farm house with a big yard that had been there for generations. It had a small concrete front porch and a long concrete sidewalk. My daughter, who was four years old at the time, was coloring on the sidewalk with those big pieces of colored chalk. I always loved seeing how creative she was. She always filled the whole sidewalk up, but she never colored on the porch. It wasn't as if she was not allowed to… she just didn't. She preferred the long sidewalk.

As I was working in the back yard, she came up to me and said, "Dad, how do you spell wait?" Not sure what she meant, I said, "You mean like wait a minute or lifting weights?" "Like wait a minute," she replied. "W-A-I-T," I said, and she went skipping back to the front of the house.

I'm not sure how long after that it was, but I remember that it was getting warm outside, so I decided to go into the house to cool off. As I walked around the side of the house toward the front porch, I saw the drawings Sara had made on the sidewalk and I smiled. As I stepped up onto the porch and toward the front door, I saw some words written in colored chalk directly in my path. I stopped dead in my tracks when I read them.

Three simple words brought me to my knees in tears... GOD IS WAITING.

I can barely even type this right now because it still brings me to tears. My God, the God of Abraham, Jacob, Daniel, David, and Elijah, used my little girl, the most precious person on the face of the Earth to me, to write a personal message to ME! My daughter could barely spell at that age, but she put those three words together so well, in a place where I had to see it. That moment changed my life forever.

"For God's gifts and <u>His call</u> are irrevocable" Romans 11:29.

God was reminding me not only of my commitment to Him, but about His patience with me, as well. I knew then that His call for my life was irrevocable. No fingers crossed. No changing of the mind. No backup plan. God had filled in that blank check when I handed it to Him, and it was time to cash it. That Sunday morning, I made my commitment public before my church. I was already working with the youth, but now it just got real. God began to stir me. I began to get deeper into the Bible and as I did, I constantly saw verses differently. I saw my own life as a teen come into full view through Scripture. It excited me and I knew that I had to share that excitement with the students of my church.

What started as a Sunday School class of four or five young people, soon blossomed into a youth group of close to fifty students hungry for the Word of God! Stop running from God and let Him bless you where you are!

Lazarus

Frank A. Jones, III

"Now when He had said these things, He cried with a loud voice, "Lazarus, come forth!" John 11:43

On the Tenth Day of November 2013, after a very eventful weekend in which God used me as an instrument to minister in multiple services, we attempted to enjoy some leisure time together with our spiritual parents at a New Orleans Saints game. Immediately when we arrived, our spiritual mother, who had years of medical experience, recognized that something was off with me and suggested that rather than following our preplanned schedule and having lunch, that I would lie down and rest before the game. Quite naturally, I submitted to her wisdom. After the game, we were scheduled to be in Houma, Louisiana which was 58 miles the equivalent of around a one hour drive from New Orleans.

Upon arrival, we immediately showered and prepared for bed. Between 3 and 5am, I began to convulse, waking my wife who immediately rose and attempted to wake me up. Unsuccessful, the seizures continued until my eyes rolled to the back of my head and I stopped breathing. She quickly dialed 911 and was instructed to do CPR until the paramedics arrived. With the aid of God, she was able to move my lifeless body to the floor and continue CPR. Finally, there was a knock on the door. They had arrived. They insisted that she leave the room while they worked on reviving me. Praise God! They were able to get a pulse! Not out of the woods yet, the paramedics quickly transported me to Terrebonne Medical for treatment. Though I had a pulse, I was still unconscious and convulsing. By this time, the word was spread through the country and the world to my brothers and sisters in Christ, as well as my beloved church, *City of Refuge*, that it was prayer time!

"When Jesus heard that, he said, This sickness is not unto death, but for the glory of God, that the Son of God might be glorified thereby" John 11:4.

Upon arriving, the physicians did extensive tests attempting to diagnose the source of the problem. Questions were asked to my wife regarding drug use, alcohol abuse, and my family's medical history whereby she replied that none of that applied to me. Finally, after around eight hours, a cardiologist arrived and revealed his findings. He shared with my family that he needed to treat me for cardiac death. "Cardiac Death?" "Yes," he replied, "... because he died!" "As a result, we must put him in a medically induced coma and pray that he wakes up. But we cannot make any promises," he said. "There is a 1 and 100 chance he will wake up and a 1 and 1000 chance that he will remember you, because we don't know how long he was without Oxygen to the brain. Now, the wait begins." The Word of God tells us to watch and pray and that's what the Body of Christ did. Twenty four hours later, they began to wake me up. Calling for the family, they gave them the news they prayed for. I was awake. I recognized my family. I was able to quote the books of the Bible. I was back. Praise be unto God, I was back to continue the work God had assigned me to. The Lazarus effect is impossible without the God factor! Hence, the Man of God that I would like to reference my Life to is the Life of *Lazarus* of Bethany.

Lazarus of Bethany is an unsung and often overlooked hero in the Word of God. His life is often mired in controversy. But as we take a closer look at him, he is a pivotal part of the testimony of Christ. Upon his birth, he was named Lazarus, or Eleazar in the Hebrew, which means *God Helped!* Isn't that befitting to someone who experienced such an amazing testimony. One would say how is it that he could be so valuable when there is not one word recorded that proceeded out of his mouth. But yet he is the focus of this time of devotion. And one that I can truly relate to. It bears saying that our lives are written epistles. And as the Gospel artists The Williams Brothers say, *we are living testimonies*. We should have been dead and gone, but God let us live on. Hallelujah!!!

Let's take a closer look at Lazarus. First, he was a part of a family that was in the inner circle of Christ. And we notice that he not only knew our Lord, but he was also known of Him on a personal level. Listen to the account of John in John 11:3-5.

"Therefore his sisters sent unto him, saying, Lord, behold, he whom thou lovest is sick. When Jesus heard that, he said, This sickness is not unto death, but for the glory of God, that the Son of God might be glorified thereby. Now Jesus loved Martha, and her sister, and Lazarus."

It is obvious that Lazarus had an intimate relationship with our Lord, but so did his sisters, Mary and Martha. So much so that they appealed to Him and almost placed a demand on that relationship during a critical time of need. They not only interceded for him, but also expressed their confidence in His love for Lazarus. Again, they prayed for Lazarus but no word is recorded of Lazarus praying for help. It reminds me again of my testimonial plight. While I was in the coma, wires in my chest and a breathing tube down my throat, when I could not pray or even knew I was in danger, someone was praying for me! I had many *Marys and Marthas*.

The Bible clearly states that Jesus not only loved Lazarus, but He also loved Martha and Mary yet His response did not reflect that statement. Because the Bible declared *He didn't move*. John 11:6 says, *"When he had heard therefore that he was sick, he abode two days still in the same place where he was."* Why do bad things happen to good men? This is an age old question but remember, there is a method to the madness, a purpose for our pain, and yes, a reason for all seasons. As I lay in that bed jerking and convulsing, not responding to the cries of my family, the petitions went up to God but the answering, initially *nothing*. But yet I know, and my family knew, that God loved me. But a greater plan was at work. We must be careful that we don't indict God prematurely when the plan of God is still in play. During this process, Lazarus' situation worsened and of course you know ultimately declined to the point of death. It has been well said that "the end of man is the beginning of God's work!" Jesus didn't move until Lazarus was dead. And yet He revealed that it was all a part of God's sovereign plan.

For three years of his public ministry, our Lord healed the sick, opened blind eyes, walked on water, transformed water to wine, and now He demonstrates His last and most resisting enemy, death. Lazarus would be a precursor testifying of the sovereign authority of God. That others would be convinced and despite what was to come at Calvary, Our Lord was the Resurrection and the Life!

My whole life has been one of grace and mercy. I lived a life in which God protected me from seen and unseen dangers because of His great love. My mother often shares with me how even as an infant, I would have seizures and the specialist could not find the root cause. I was very active as a young man playing basketball, and even a little football. Physicals twice a year even as an adult. But after being raised from the dead, they diagnosed me with cardiomyopathy. My heart was enlarged. When I consider athletes such as Hank Gathers and Conrad Mcray that died playing the sport that they love, I am even more appreciative of the grace of God to live. Being one that has had the privilege to experience physical resurrection elevates you to awe at the grandeur and power of God. Thus, removing all fear of the uncertainties of life. This causes you to confront all danger with faith, declaring with God *nothing shall be impossible*, Luke 1:37.

But one might say, "I've never been physically deceased, how can I relate to such a plight?" And my response would be *but yet you have*. Every born again believer can attest to the fact that before their encounter with God, they were spiritually deceased. Living, but yet lifeless. Until that fateful day that we accepted Christ and spiritually resuscitated, now we are living witnesses of His power. We can attest to the fact that there is life after death. Regardless of the situation, the potential and power of God to give it a *Lazarus* experience is yet available.

As a preacher and teacher of the Word of God, I have not only experienced, but also witnessed this power in the lives of the faithful. I guess you can call me an eye witness to His miracle working power. We often ask God to use us for His glory. We declare that we are available to Him. But we want to choose our order. We want to tell God how and where we would like to be used. The scripture says that the steps of a good man are ORDERED by the Lord. Similar to Lazarus, those orders are not always pleasant, but necessary. Listen to the words of Peter in regards to suffering in 1 Peter 4:14:

"If ye be reproached for the name of Christ, happy are ye; for the spirit of glory and of God resteth upon you: on their part he is evil spoken of, but on your part he is glorified."

The Greek says, "the Spirit of Glory and that of God." Meaning, the Spirit of Glory is God and the One whom through the power of His resurrection of Christ was glorified. Everything in Creation has the potential to bring glory to God. Psalm 19 reveals that even the heavens declare the Glory of God. And there is embryonic potential in each of us.

Lastly, to those who have had a Lazarus experience. Be aware that the experience marks you and causes you to be labeled "Armed and Dangerous" due to the fact you are a living testimony. Yes, you are a threat to the plans of Satan. Even our Lord declared that the last enemy that would be destroyed would be death. But yet this mark, or testimony, speaks of His supremacy over that which plagued man since the fall of humanity. Listen to the account of John regarding Lazarus' life after his resurrection.

"Much people of the Jews therefore knew that he was there: and they came not for Jesus' sake only, but that they might see Lazarus also, whom he had raised from the dead. But the chief priests consulted that they might put Lazarus also to death; Because that by reason of him many of the Jews went away, and believed on Jesus" John 12:9-11.

How amazing and powerful the Life and Legacy of Lazarus had become. His very existence threatened the chief priests because he had become a great attraction. A Living Bible. To the point that they planned to put him to death because he became instrumental in the conversion of their colleagues.

According to the Eastern Orthodox church, after the resurrection of Christ, Lazarus would be forced to flee for his life to Cyprus and be ordained as the first Bishop of Kiton. Without speaking one word, his life, like yours, speaks of God's power. But yet your testimony does not cease; it opens doors for you and I to give more glory to God. Because as was a desire of the Apostle Paul fulfilled in your life:

"That I may know him, and the power of his resurrection," Philippians 3:10.

Meet the Author

Chris Hunter, Jr. is a retired Army veteran of 25 years. Chris is the Founder of Hunter Entertainment Network, a merger of Hunter Heart Publishing and Christ HuNterz Productions, a book publishing and music and movie production company. Chris works for the government at the United States Air Force Academy. He holds an Bachelor's Degree in Business, and an Associate's in Cyber Security and Culinary Arts. He is also a licensed barber.

Chris is married to Deborah G. Hunter and together, they have six children and five grandchildren. They live in the beautiful mountains of Colorado.